The SUFFERING
and VICTORIOUS
CHRIST

The SUFFERING and VICTORIOUS CHRIST

Toward a More Compassionate Christology

RICHARD J. MOUW
and DOUGLAS A. SWEENEY

Baker Academic
a division of Baker Publishing Group
Grand Rapids, Michigan

Published by Baker Academic
a division of Baker Publishing Group
P.O. Box 6287, Grand Rapids, MI 49516-6287
www.bakeracademic.com

Printed in the United States of America

Library of Congress Cataloging-in-Publication Data
Mouw, Richard J.
    The suffering and victorious Christ : toward a more compassionate Christology
  / Richard J. Mouw and Douglas A. Sweeney
        pages cm
    Includes bibliographical references and index.
    ISBN 978-0-8010-4844-9 (pbk.)
    1. Jesus Christ—Servanthood. 2. Jesus Christ—Person and offices. I. Title.
BT257.M68 2013
232—dc23   2013004888

13 14 15 16 17 18 19   7 6 5 4 3 2 1

To
Walter Hansen,
cherished colleague, dear friend, and
great supporter of global theological fellowship

Contents

Acknowledgments

This book would not exist without the encouragement and help we have received from many others. First and foremost, we offer thanks to the organizers, hosts, and fellow participants at the conference "Suffering and Hope in Jesus Christ: Christological Polarity and Religious Pluralism," cosponsored by Trinity's Henry Center and Tokyo Christian University. Spearheaded by Harold Netland, administered ably by Owen Strachan and the marvelous staff at Tokyo Christian, hosted marvelously by President Masanori Kurasawa and Dean Takanori Kobayashi, this was a wonderful environment in which to conceive a book. Our fellow speakers at the conference—Hisakazu Inagaki, Shohei Yamato, Akio Ito, Anri Morimoto, Heon-Wook Park, Graham Cole, Nelson Jennings, Richard Bauckham, and Tite Tiénou—were fantastic interlocutors.

After the conference was over, we received additional help from an expert team of editorial colleagues. Bob Hosack kindly agreed to shepherd our project at Baker Academic. Brandon O'Brien and David Barshinger helped us turn two conference papers into a small but substantive book. Harold Netland, David Kirkpatrick, Hans Madueme, David Luy, Jimmy Byrd, and Alan Watt gave the manuscript attention, offering valuable commentary and encouragement. Earlier versions of some of our chapters and/or queries from the authors were read and responded to insightfully by Paul Harvey, Scott Manetsch, Mickey Mattox, Joel Okamoto, and Beth Schweiger.

Last but not least, Walter Hansen has helped in too many ways to count. He enabled the Tokyo conference, read the papers we presented, encouraged the book you hold in your hands, and has proven himself an indispensable partner over and over, both at Fuller and at Trinity. We dedicate this book to him as a token of our admiration and gratitude.

Introduction

We began to think about writing this book after presenting papers together at a conference held at Tokyo Christian University in the summer of 2010. We joined with eight other scholars—from Japan, Korea, Britain, Australia, and the United States—to explore what we could learn from one another about pain and suffering, victory and hope, as they relate to the significance of Jesus Christ in our globalizing and pluralistic world. We wanted to play from our strengths and work with familiar resources, so we turned to our respective theological traditions for guidance toward a more global and compassionate Christology.

On the surface, our Japanese interlocutors appeared to have a longer-established tradition of theology that takes seriously the suffering of the Lord. In his novel *The Samurai* (1980), the celebrated Japanese Roman Catholic writer Shusaku Endo suggests that the Japanese have held a *Christus dolor* theology since the advent of the faith in that country in the early seventeenth century. One of his characters says of Jesus:

> He understands the hearts of the wretched, because his entire life was wretched. He knows the agonies of those who die a miserable death, because he died in misery. He was not in the least powerful. He was not beautiful. . . . He never visited the houses of those who were puffed up or contented. He sought out only the ugly, the wretched, the miserable and the sorrowful. But now even the [European] bishops and priests

here are complacent and swollen with pride. They are no longer the sort of people He sought after.[1]

Whether or not this quotation expresses the perspective of seventeenth-century Japanese Christians, it reflects modern Japanese critiques of Western Christology.[2] For more than half a century, well-known Japanese Christian writers have noted the masculine triumphalism of Western Christianity—especially among Americans, like us.[3] Long before World War II, Kanzō Uchimura, a Japanese writer and teacher who founded his nation's so-called Nonchurch Movement, claimed that Westerners distorted the peaceful doctrine of Jesus Christ. "Christianity in the West has become an anomaly," he said. Westerners "love to fight. . . . So when they adopted Christianity, they made it a fighting religion, an [*sic*] European and American religion, entirely contrary to its original genius. As an Asiatic religion," he continued by way of contrast, "Christianity is a war-hater, war-curser, and war-abolisher; but these Europe-Americans, as they could not deny their inborn warlife [*sic*] nature, made Christianity a warlike religion."[4] After the horror of World War II, other Japanese Christian writers added their voices to what soon became a chorus of concern. These critics worried that Western militarism led Americans to highlight God and Jesus Christ's power, stringent holiness, and victory over sin far above their passion, condescension to our weaknesses, and identification with abject human suffering.

By contrast, Asian theologians have consistently emphasized the suffering and brokenness of Christ. Kazoh Kitamori, a Lutheran

---

1. Shusaku Endo, *The Samurai*, trans. Van C. Gessel (New York: New Directions Books, 1982; orig. Japanese ed., 1980), 220–21.

2. It is important to note, however, that not all Japanese thinkers share Shusaku Endo's views. It might be said, in fact, that Endo is more beloved among non-Christians there than among his fellow Christians, who oppose what they take to be his suggestion that Christianity cannot grow in Japan without fundamental change, that one cannot be fully Christian and also fully Japanese.

3. We use labels such as "Japanese," "Western," and "American" theology advisedly, largely because they are used in the literature we engage. Uncomfortable with essentializing language such as this, recognizing its inadequacy to account for the rich variety of theologies "East" and "West," we devote this little book in part to problematizing the ongoing use of such abstractions and improving our understanding of the views they represent.

4. Kanzō Uchimura, "Christianity and Buddhism," in *The Complete Works of Kanzō Uchimura*, vol. 4, *The Japan Christian Intelligencer* (Tokyo: Kyobunkwan, 1972), 59.

theologian, spent his life emphasizing what he called "the pain of God" within a theology of the cross that How Chuang Chua describes aptly as a "*Dolor Dei*" doctrine—a doctrine of the suffering and sorrow of the Lord—that speaks prophetically against theologies of glory found so often in the West.[5] Kosuke Koyama, in *Mount Fuji and Mount Sinai* (1985), repeated this refrain, calling readers everywhere to rectify the doctrinal balance that was lost amid the triumph of the Western *Christus victor.* "In our modern [Western] context," Koyama postulated,

> we are tempted to speak more positively about an unbroken Christ, a powerful, conquering Christ. Christian theology, under the influence of the Greek philosophical mind and the Latin administrative mind, has become largely a theology of the unbroken Christ. The theological meaning of the brokenness in the depth of the work and person of Jesus Christ has been ignored. Both philosophical and administrative minds are attracted to the concept of "perfection" and they dislike "brokenness." Indeed, we question whether we can find hope in the broken Christ. How can we trust in such a "weak," even repelling, image of Christ? A strong Western civilization and the "weak" Christ cannot be reconciled harmoniously. Christ must become "strong." A strong United States and a strong Christ! . . . Yet in speaking about the broken Christ, we are speaking about creation, construction, integration, reconciliation and healing. We are listening now to the ancient words of the Bible, "he was bruised for our iniquities; upon him was the chastisement that made us whole" (Isa. 53:5). The image of the broken Christ comes to us every time we approach the Lord's Supper. As it is this broken Christ who exposes human idolatry.[6]

Shusaku Endo emphasized the need in Japan for ways of speaking of God that pay due heed to the theme of suffering in God, Jesus Christ,

5. Kazoh Kitamori, *Theology of the Pain of God* (Richmond, VA: John Knox, 1965; orig. Japanese ed., 1946); and How Chuang Chua, "Japanese Perspectives on the Death of Christ: A Study in Contextualized Christology" (PhD diss., Trinity Evangelical Divinity School, 2007), 184, 197.

6. Kosuke Koyama, *Mount Fuji and Mount Sinai: A Critique of Idols* (Maryknoll, NY: Orbis Books, 1985), 242. These critiques have critics of their own. See especially Akio Hashimoto, "Legacy of Kitamori in Contemporary Japanese Christian Thought," *Missio Apostolica: Journal of the Lutheran Society for Missiology* 12 (May 2004): 11–16; and Chua, "Japanese Perspectives on the Death of Christ," who discusses Kitamori's critique of Endo (257–63) and his own critique of Endo (274–83). The entire issue of *Missio Apostolica* cited above is devoted to an engagement with Kitamori.

and those who walk the way of the cross. "The religious mentality of the Japanese is . . . responsive to one who 'suffers with us,'" Endo wrote, "and who 'allows for our weakness.'" The Japanese, moreover, "tend to seek in their gods and buddhas a warm-hearted mother" more than a distant, "stern father."[7] In order to hear the Christian message, they must know that God is more than just a righteous heavenly Father who is angry over sin; God is also One who loves and draws near in times of need.

Asian concerns about American Christian triumphalism are not unfounded. After all, theologians and other leaders in the United States had indeed called for a more masculine Jesus to bolster the nation in its time of distress before, during, and after the World Wars. "The men of a strenuous age demand a strenuous Christ," argued R. Warren Conant in his 1915 book *The Virility of Christ: A New View*. "If they fail to find him the church is to blame. For Christ himself was strenuous enough to satisfy the most exacting; he was stalwart and fearless, aggressive and progressive; never flinching from a challenge, overwhelming in quickness and sharpness of attack; yet withal wary and wise, never 'rattled,' always holding himself well in hand."[8] Conant's message found an eager audience. Jonathan Ebel reports that Conant's "view of Christ as an active, often militant man, fed the early-twentieth-century growth of intra- and extra-ecclesial Christian organizations designed to attract and retain young men with a strenuous Christian faith."[9]

Moreover, the criticisms of our Asian brothers and sisters have been echoed by writers in the United States who worry about the glib, exultant, protean views of Jesus that have been easy to enlist in support of Western secular values and that have been used to stoke the "Captain America complex."[10] Stephen Nichols complains in his

---

7. Shusaku Endo, *A Life of Jesus*, trans. Richard A. Schuchert (New York: Paulist Press, 1978; orig. Japanese ed., 1973), 1. Endo's best-known novel, *Silence* (trans. William Johnston [New York: Taplinger, 1969]), deals extensively with the protagonist's feeling that the Western God is silent in the face of human suffering. Endo also deals at length with the question of God's passion in *The Samurai* and in *Deep River*, trans. Van C. Gessel (New York: New Directions, 1994).

8. R. Warren Conant, *The Virility of Christ: A New View* (Chicago: n.p., 1915), 29.

9. Jonathan H. Ebel, *Faith in the Fight: Religion and the American Soldier in the Great War* (Princeton: Princeton University Press, 2010), 8.

10. See Robert Jewett and John Shelton Lawrence, *Captain America and the Crusade against Evil: The Dilemma of Zealous Nationalism* (Grand Rapids: Eerdmans, 2003).

book *Jesus Made in America* (2008) that fellow North Americans, especially evangelicals, have all too often "settled for a Christology that can be reduced to a bumper sticker."[11] Harry Stout contends further that such superficial boosterism has fanned "America's faith in the institution of war as a divine instrument and sacred mandate to be exercised around the world. . . . Without religion," Stout suggests, "the institution of war could not have thrived in American history. Religion not only provided an overarching meaning to America as 'exceptional,' and 'messianic,' it also contributed to the blind eye Americans have cast toward their nation's myriad military adventures."[12]

Recent research by Jonathan Ebel supports Stout's observations on the relationship between religion and bellicosity in America. Ebel argues that "religion was not merely a marginal or secondary concern in the American experience of the Great War. American involvement in the war began and ended with talk of redemption."[13] Ebel doubts America ever would have entered the war were it not for its uniquely religious identity:

> American experiences of the war were suffused with religion to the extent that we must at least consider the notion that without the prevalence of masculinized Christianity and the many subtler ways that Christian or Judeo-Christian ideas informed Americans' attachments to one another, the nation, and the cause, American involvement in the war would not have been possible. Framed as a question, while religion clearly shaped soldiers' and war workers' experiences of combat and sustained many in war's midst, was it religion that put them there in the first place? Though one can and should argue this question both ways, I will cast my lot with those who argue the affirmative.[14]

11. Stephen J. Nichols, *Jesus Made in America: A Cultural History from the Puritans to "The Passion of the Christ"* (Downers Grove, IL: IVP Academic, 2008), 18.

12. Harry S. Stout, "Review Essay: Religion, War, and the Meaning of America," *Religion and American Culture: A Journal of Interpretation* 19 (Summer 2009): 284. For more on the cultural history of American views of Jesus, see especially Stephen Prothero, *American Jesus: How the Son of God Became a National Icon* (New York: Farrar, Straus & Giroux, 2003); and Richard Wightman Fox, *Jesus in America: Personal Savior, Cultural Hero, National Obsession* (San Francisco: HarperSanFrancisco, 2004). Greater attention to doctrinal history may be found in Bruce M. Stephens, *The Prism of Time and Eternity: Images of Christ in American Protestant Thought from Jonathan Edwards to Horace Bushnell*, ATLA Monograph Series (Lanham, MD: Scarecrow Press, 1996).

13. Ebel, *Faith in the Fight*, 193.

14. Ibid., 194.

Ebel goes on to suggest, without stating this explicitly, that other American wars have been intimately tied up with Christianity, especially since the Civil War: "The centrality of religion to the American experience of the Great War and the many ways in which religion shaped soldiers' and war workers' actions and perceptions will and should invite comparisons to other more and less storied wars and the religious lives of the Americans who wage them."[15]

Engaging Christology from Reformation Traditions

As incisive—and as fair—as the criticisms of our Asian brothers are, we are convinced there are many important exceptions to this kind of bellicosity. Not all American Christians have such glib and exultant views of their relationship to God and, through Christ, to the rest of the world. Today, many American Christians have begun to expand their view of the work of God throughout the world. Some of our theologians are now listening to and engaging with non-Western Christian leaders.[16]

15. Ibid., 195. On this theme, see also the recent work of James P. Byrd, *Sacred Scripture, Sacred War: The Bible and the American Revolution* (New York: Oxford University Press, 2013); and Andrew Preston, *Sword of the Spirit, Shield of Faith: Religion in American War and Diplomacy* (New York: Alfred A. Knopf, 2012), who demonstrates that "religion has had an almost uniquely intimate relationship with American war and diplomacy. In times of war, religious liberals and conservatives, militants and pacifists, have all called upon God to sanctify their cause, and all have viewed America as God's chosen land. As a result, U.S. foreign policy has often acquired the tenor of a moral crusade" (4).

16. Recent calls from the United States for a more global Christian perspective on the part of theologians include Craig Ott and Harold A. Netland, eds., *Globalizing Theology: Belief and Practice in an Era of World Christianity* (Grand Rapids: Baker Academic, 2006); Timothy C. Tennent, *Theology in the Context of World Christianity: How the Global Church Is Influencing the Way We Think about and Discuss Theology* (Grand Rapids: Zondervan, 2007); and Jeffrey P. Greenman and Gene L. Green, eds., *Global Theology in Evangelical Perspective: Exploring the Contextual Nature of Theology and Mission* (Downers Grove, IL: IVP Academic, 2012). The best example of a book that is changing the way North Americans think about Christology is written by a Canadian, Diane B. Stinton, *Jesus of Africa: Voices of Contemporary African Christology*, Faith and Cultures Series (Maryknoll, NY: Orbis Books, 2004). These books echo calls deriving from numerous African Christian sources, most famously the work of the late Kwame Bediako, *Jesus and the Gospel in Africa: History and Experience*, Theology in Africa Series (Maryknoll, NY: Orbis Books, 2004). See also Vinay Samuel and Chris Sugden, eds., *Sharing Jesus in the Two Thirds World: Evangelical Christologies from the Contexts of Poverty, Powerlessness and Religious Pluralism* (Grand Rapids: Eerdmans, 1983); and Daniel Lucas Lukito,

More to the point, we are not convinced that violence, triumphalism, and denial of the suffering of God are essential to the Reformation traditions. We readily admit that the traditions have their limitations. Indeed, the reason we set out on this project is because of our awareness of the limitations of our traditions. We acknowledge that they should be saying more, should be addressing issues and themes that, historically, they have not. Nevertheless, we are committed to these traditions—Douglas Sweeney to Lutheranism and Richard Mouw to Calvinism—because we believe they do, in fact, speak meaningfully in orthodox and scholastic terms about the significance of the suffering of Christ and the association of God, through Christ, with the marginalized. Our challenge, then, is to determine how to open up these traditions so that they speak to the concerns of the global Christian church without violating their essential elements and commitments.

And Asian Christians are not our only interlocutors in this regard. We have also been listening to a younger generation of our evangelical contemporaries, many of whom are dissatisfied with the kind of theology they have inherited from their spiritual forebears. In recent years they have expressed their dissatisfaction, for example, with various theories of the atonement. Many of these younger Christian leaders—some of whom even insist on wearing the label "post-evangelical"—are wanting to downplay, and even in some cases firmly reject, the "forensic" and "individualistic" ideas associated with the traditional adherence to doctrines such as the penal substitutionary atonement.

Our own Lutheran and Calvinist loyalties do not incline us to share in that dissatisfaction. But we have tried to understand it, and we are convinced that this development is not simply motivated by a thoroughgoing rejection of traditional teachings. Indeed, many who express this frustration are looking deep into ancient traditions— the theologies of the Eastern Orthodox Churches, for example—for plausible alternatives.

Our sense is that the dissatisfaction with standard evangelical atonement emphases stems, in part, from a concern, confirmed by some recent sociological studies, that many younger evangelicals worry about a widespread image of the North American evangelical community as intolerant, judgmental, and given to polarizing attitudes. If

Making Christology Relevant to the Third World: Applying Christopraxis to Local Struggle, European University Studies (Bern: Peter Lang, 1998).

we put this cultural worry together with the quest for a less "forensic" view of the redemptive mission of Christ, we can, we think, discern an underlying desire for the very thing we want to explore in this book: a more compassionate Christology. And again, we are not ready to reject those features of the work of Christ that the evangelical movement has so centrally emphasized due to its theological formation by the sixteenth-century Reformation, but we are convinced that we need to give much more attention than our traditions historically have to the ways in which God's plan of the incarnation arose in large part from his desire to enter into the frailties, fears, and agonies of the human condition in the person of Jesus of Nazareth.

Our Approach in This Book

To make our case, we will look for elements in our traditions— admittedly very often underplayed—that point to divine empathy. But we will also look at one important Christian community on our own continent that gives us much to work with theologically as we pursue our goals. Through hymns, sermons, and personal narratives, black Christians in America have testified both to a *Christus victor*, the great liberator from oppression, and a *Christus dolor*, the man of sorrows who bore the yoke of slavery with them. This rich literature provides a strong counterpoint to the "masculine triumphalism" of much so-called traditional—and white—American Christology. Our research confirmed for us that, in many important ways, the African American christological tradition resonates with and develops traditional Reformational resources. It articulates, often more colorfully and compellingly, the concepts of association and suffering and incarnation burrowed in our own more scholastic traditions. And it makes clear the central challenge that faces the theologian in search of a more compassionate Christology: joining Christ's immanence to his transcendence. Like our Japanese colleagues, the African American churches speak powerfully and meaningfully about the lowly, broken Christ who meets humans in their need, and in so doing, they alert us to the danger of presenting Christ, in his perfections, as distant from human experience.

While we recognize the limitations of our Reformation traditions and the strengths of other traditions in articulating the kind of Christology we seek, we also think Japan needs Nicaea and that the African

American churches need the Reformation. The Reformers help us—all of us—think through important theological and practical aspects of our faith. We are engaged, then, in a project of critique. But we believe critique must be a moment, not a way of life.[17] Our question, then, is, How can we articulate a more compassionate and globally relevant Christology in terms that are faithful to and consistent with the Reformation traditions we claim, but are also disciplined by the concerns and experiences of our Asian and non-European brothers and sisters?

The chapters that follow represent our humble effort to answer this question. The content of this book is based on the research we undertook in preparation for the conference in Japan and borrows from the papers we delivered there. But much of it is the result of our further reflection on how to bring our theological traditions into conversation with an African American christological tradition in order to articulate a new normative "American" Christology for a global age. In the pages that follow, we explore several theological resources, all from the time when our theology was coming into its own, and when most theologians still assumed the responsibility of thinking *with the church* (and thus can help us do so now).[18] Some of them will be familiar; others will not. Some of them are American; others are not. Some were slaves; others were their masters. Some of them were scholars; others were illiterate. All of them testify to the fact that even in the nineteenth and early twentieth centuries, Christians

17. We borrow this phrase from the title of C. Stephen Evans's book, *Despair, a Moment or a Way of Life?* (Downers Grove, IL: InterVarsity, 1971).

18. There are others in this period who might have been considered. Most importantly, Horace Bushnell (1802–1876) addressed this subject, going so far as to teach that God himself suffers with humanity: "God suffers on account of evil, or with and for created beings under evil—a fact very commonly disallowed and rejected, I am sorry to add, even by Christian theology itself, as being rationally irreconcilable with God's greatness and sufficiency." Bushnell was a maverick, however, whose understanding of this matter "excludes the possibility . . . of any dogmatic formula, in which it may be adequately stated." In fact, Bushnell was a harsh critic of all confessional, dogmatic, even systematic theology. He did not invest heavily in the task of exegesis, or historical theology, or dialogue with others who were wrestling with his issues. Though tremendously important in the rise of Protestant liberalism (and other Christian movements), he is far less helpful than even poor and illiterate slaves as a conversation partner for Christians today trying to think with the communion of the saints. See especially Horace Bushnell, *The Vicarious Sacrifice, Grounded in Principles of Universal Obligation* (New York: Scribner, 1866), 223–30 (quotations from 223, 213).

were wrestling with the suffering of God, the death of God in Christ, and the Lord's identification with our weakness and affliction. And all of them can help us complement the *Christus victor* (Christ the victor) with an American *Christus dolor* (One who suffered and is sorrowful) to establish a global *Christus dolor* who ministers to those acquainted with brokenness and grief.[19]

The first four chapters deal with resources from our own theological heritages. In the work of Reformed theologian John Williamson Nevin, we see how moving the incarnation to the center of theological discourse provides a means of talking about Jesus's descent into, assumption of, and association with the human condition. Lutheran theologian Franz Pieper goes a step further and predicates suffering of God himself by speaking powerfully about the suffering of God in the suffering of Jesus. Together, Nevin and Pieper can help us promote a Christology of suffering with greater courage. Moreover, Pieper provides the systematic theological framework that will help make sense of traditional African American Christology as it is here described. In addition, a comparison of Roman Catholic and Reformed theologies will reveal that the Reformed tradition has sufficient resources of its own through doctrines such as creation and nature to express God's identification with humanity. Finally, representatives of the Reformed tradition, including Charles Hodge, will remind us of the importance of preserving the uniqueness of Jesus's suffering. If Nevin invites us to emphasize the suffering of Jesus and Pieper encourages us to speak more boldly of the suffering God, others in the Reformed tradition remind us of the important limits within which this conversation should take place. Moreover, the christological differences between Pieper and Hodge reflect the differences in the Lutheran and Reformed

---

19. Of course, the doctrine of *Christus victor* is not American in origin. Nor is it always used aggressively. The Swedish churchman Gustaf Aulén gave the doctrine its greatest currency as he argued for what he called the "classical" view of the atonement, found in Irenaeus and Luther, in which Christ conquered the worldly powers of sin, death, and the devil, reconciling the world to God through his kenotic incarnation, death, and glorious resurrection. More recently, it has been modified by the pacifist Denny Weaver, who appropriates what he calls a revised "narrative *Christus Victor*," which he offers as a nonviolent, Anabaptist, and more ethical alternative to Aulén. See Gustaf Aulén, *Christus Victor: An Historical Study of the Three Main Types of the Idea of Atonement*, trans. A. G. Hebert (New York: Macmillan, 1969); Gustaf Aulén, *The Faith of the Christian Church*, trans. Eric H. Wahlstrom (Philadelphia: Muhlenberg Press, 1960), 182–290; and J. Denny Weaver, *The Nonviolent Atonement* (Grand Rapids: Eerdmans, 2001).

traditions that we call home. We will use them in part here to establish
the traditional, Reformational concerns that typically animate and
regulate the work of white Protestants like us.

In chapter 5 we consider the Christology of Sojourner Truth and
other representative African Americans of the nineteenth century.
Following the tradition of "Negro spirituals" of the slave era, Truth
spoke with conviction about Jesus sharing in the suffering of black
folk because of his own incarnational self-emptying. She believed in
the triumphant power of God in Christ. But like her fellow subjected
people, she emphasized Christ's suffering not only on the cross but
also in the general human experience. Truth's Christology, and that
of other black writers we discuss in this chapter, moves us beyond
the systematic and theoretical and offers a set of fruitful models of
application. Even so, because Truth spent her childhood in a Dutch
Reformed community, she provides an interesting and concrete point
of intersection between the Euro-American and African American
traditions.

But applying *Christus dolor* has its challenges, an issue we take up
in chapter 6. Many black Christians modeled an appropriate identification with the sufferings of Christ, but others used that identification to justify violence and bloody triumphalism. Similarly, some
white Southerners applied the suffering of Christ to the "Lost Cause"
ideology, suggesting that the plight of the South after the Civil War
was an antitype of the humiliation of Jesus. Meanwhile, other white
Southerners who rejected the Lost Cause ideology claimed that they
were the suffering righteous who bore the stripes of Jesus. This discussion illustrates the need to move beyond the basic principle that
Jesus is always and unconditionally on the side of those who suffer.

Finally, we conclude by offering some synthesizing remarks. Looking back over the terrain we have traveled together, we make our
recommendations for what a new and more compassionate American
Christology ought to look like.

Please accept this volume as an effort to articulate a new and more
compassionate American Christology. We recognize our need to be
corrected, and we are thinking out loud. We undertake this journey of
discovery with the help of others and hope our conversation can help
others do the same. Most of all, we hope to promote a view of Jesus
that is catholic, evangelical, sensitive to the priorities of non-Western
thinkers, and edifying to those who follow Jesus in his suffering, living
cruciform lives to the glory of God.

1

John Williamson Nevin
and the Incarnation of God

Christology is complicated. It is not for the faint of heart. It considers how Jesus of Nazareth could have been both God and man and involves related questions, such as how the Son of God governed the world while in the manger (Col. 1:17; Heb. 1:3); really "increased in wisdom and in years, and in divine and human favor" (Luke 2:52); was actually tempted by the devil; truly suffered and died for us; and even unites the human race, through the church, with God himself (John 17; Eph. 2; 2 Peter 1:4; etc.).

There have been seasons of church history when such questions stood at the center of theological attention. During the fourth and fifth centuries, Christian leaders developed rules for speaking of Jesus's personality in a series of church councils called to combat a string of heresies confusing the people of God. (Arianism, Apollinarianism, Nestorianism, and Eutychianism received the most attention, though other "isms" also rankled.)[1] During the Reformation period, the Lutherans and the Reformed debated christological matters during their

---

1. The first seven of the ecumenical councils (325–787, all in modern-day Turkey) dealt with Christology. The first four of these (325–451) are best known and embraced by most Christians—Catholic, Orthodox, and Protestant. See the *Decrees of the*

battles over the mode of Christ's presence in the Eucharist.[2] During
the early modern period, scholars reapplied the earlier christological
decisions in various efforts to resolve reheated christological problems:
the Puritans, for example, fought both Quaker and Socinian views of
Jesus's personality; English theologians defended the deity of Christ
against a resurgent Arianism and deistic criticisms of traditional su-
pernaturalism; and conservatives resisted Unitarianism at Harvard,
in the Massachusetts churches, and in outposts farther south.[3]

For most of early American history, though, Protestants occupied
themselves with other, more "practical" matters. Enlightenment critics
of Christianity discouraged precarious probes into the mysteries of
faith, metaphysical conundrums, and divisive points of dogma. Be-
sides, the evangelical clergy had more basic work to do—souls to win,
churches to plant, more urgent teachings to impart. They focused on
grace and free will, original sin and true conversion, Christian piety
and devotion. Even elite theologians spent the lion's share of their time

Ecumenical Councils, vol. 1, *Nicaea I to Lateran V*, ed. Norman P. Tanner (London:
Sheed & Ward, 1990), 1–156.

2. Helpful surveys of these battles may be found in B. A. Gerrish, "Eucharist," in
The Oxford Encyclopedia of the Reformation, ed. Hans J. Hillerbrand (New York:
Oxford University Press, 1996), 2:71–81; and Lee Palmer Wandel, *The Eucharist in
the Reformation: Incarnation and Liturgy* (Cambridge: Cambridge University Press,
2006). On the Christology of the sixteenth-century Lutherans and the Reformed, start
with E. David Willis, *Calvin's Catholic Christology: The Function of the So-Called
"Extra-Calvinisticum,"* Studies in Medieval and Reformation Thought (Leiden: Brill,
1966); Ian D. Kingston Siggins, *Martin Luther's Doctrine of Christ*, Yale Publications
in Religion (New Haven: Yale University Press, 1970); Marc Lienhard, *Luther, Witness
to Jesus Christ: Stages and Themes of the Reformer's Christology*, trans. Edwin H.
Robertson (1973; Minneapolis: Augsburg, 1982); Richard A. Muller, *Christ and the
Decree: Christology and Predestination in Reformed Theology from Calvin to Perkins*
(Durham, NC: Labyrinth Press, 1986); Stephen Emondson, *Calvin's Christology*
(Cambridge: Cambridge University Press, 2004); and Oswald Bayer and Benjamin
Gleede, eds., *Creator est Creatura: Luthers Christologie als Lehre von der Idiomenkom-
munikation*, Theologische Bibliothek Töpelmann (Berlin: Walter De Gruyter, 2007).

3. On these developments, much has been written. Start with Conrad Wright, *The
Beginnings of Unitarianism in America* (Boston: Starr King Press, 1955); Maurice
Wiles, *Archetypal Heresy: Arianism through the Centuries* (Oxford: Oxford University
Press, 1996); Thomas C. Pfizenmaier, *The Trinitarian Theology of Dr. Samuel Clarke
(1675–1729): Context, Sources, and Controversy*, Studies in the History of Christian
Thought (Leiden: Brill, 1997); Carl R. Trueman, *The Claims of Truth: John Owen's
Trinitarian Theology* (Carlisle, UK: Paternoster, 1998); Alan Spence, *Incarnation and
Inspiration: John Owen and the Coherence of Christology* (London: T&T Clark, 2007)
and Paul C. H. Lim, *Mystery Unveiled: The Crisis of the Trinity in Early Modern
England* (New York: Oxford University Press, 2012).

stemming the tide of skepticism and the religion of nature and reason, emphasizing the weight of evidence for their supernatural claims and stressing humanity's need for revelation. They looked for support, inspiration, and rhetorical resources to the inductive, scientific method of England's Francis Bacon and the empirical philosophy of England's John Locke. As Brooks Holifield contends in his magisterial survey of American theology, "a majority of theologians in early America shared a preoccupation with the reasonableness of Christianity that predisposed them toward" a rational and sober "understanding of theology."[4] Their feet were firmly planted in solid, actionable intelligence, in doctrines that pertained directly to basic Christian faith and its defense in an increasingly hostile age. Few would spare much time for more mysterious inquiries into the union of humanity with God in Jesus Christ, and, when they did, they usually rehearsed the standard formulas inherited from Protestant scholastics. These inquiries never vanished. They remained a major locus of traditional Christian faith, and most professional theologians felt a need to come to terms with them. But christological matters failed to gain significant traction and find much momentum in American theology until well into the antebellum period.

German Thought in America

By about the 1840s, things began to change. And they did so under the influence of John Williamson Nevin (1803–1886) and the Mercersburg Theology of the German Reformed Church. Nevin was not alone in shifting his gaze to other subjects in this period of transition. Rather, as Claude Welch has clarified, his shift belonged to a trend during "the middle third of the century" when "the Christological problem came to the center of the stage," providing "a focus for . . . other concerns" in Western theological circles.[5] It was also part of a larger trend away from evidentialist, conversionist theology shaped by British empirical thought to transcendental, churchly doctrine

4. E. Brooks Holifield, *Theology in America: Christian Thought from the Age of the Puritans to the Civil War* (New Haven: Yale University Press, 2003), 4. On the main lines of early American theological work, see also Mark A. Noll, *America's God: From Jonathan Edwards to Abraham Lincoln* (New York: Oxford University Press, 2002).

5. Claude Welch, *Protestant Thought in the Nineteenth Century*, vol. 1, *1799–1870* (New Haven: Yale University Press, 1972), 145.

shaped by German romanticism and idealism. But Nevin and his work personified and spread these movements most forcefully in America. Although reared by Presbyterians and trained at Princeton Seminary—by Charles Hodge and others who were devoted to Britain's Westminster Confession and catechisms—he later joined the German Reformed Church and turned to more Germanic forms of thought, opposed to what he considered the grubbing positivism and rationalism of modern American "Puritanism" (a term he used loosely to refer to modern evangelical Protestantism generally).[6]

Germanic forms of thought were all the rage in the 1840s, the leading fashion among the avant-garde American literati.[7] Many *Anglo-*American readers found them threatening and subversive. Many patriots, in fact, affirmed the stereotypes promoted by men like Edward Robinson—a scholar at Andover Seminary who had studied at length in Germany and married a German woman—who said that Germans were "a people of comparatively little practical energy, but of vast intellectual exertion."[8] In America, of course, impractical thought was often derided. From the founding of the country, national leaders

6. For more on Nevin's life and thought (as well as the Mercersburg Theology), see D. G. Hart, *John Williamson Nevin: High-Church Calvinist*, American Reformed Biographies (Phillipsburg, NJ: P&R, 2005); William DiPuccio, *The Interior Sense of Scripture: The Sacred Hermeneutics of John W. Nevin*, Studies in American Biblical Hermeneutics (Macon, GA: Mercer University Press, 1998); Richard E. Wentz, *John Williamson Nevin: American Theologian*, Religion in America Series (New York: Oxford University Press, 1997); Sam Hamstra, Jr., and Arie J. Griffioen, eds., *Reformed Confessionalism in Nineteenth-Century America: Essays on the Thought of John Williamson Nevin*, ATLA Monograph Series (Lanham, MD: Scarecrow, 1995); James Hastings Nichols, *Romanticism in American Theology: Nevin and Schaff at Mercersburg* (Chicago: University of Chicago Press, 1961); Theodore Appel, *The Life and Work of John Williamson Nevin* (Philadelphia: Reformed Church Publication House, 1889); E. V. Gerhart, "John Williamson Nevin: His Godliness," *The Reformed Quarterly Review* 34 (January 1887): 13–19; and especially John W. Nevin, *My Own Life: The Earliest Years* (Lancaster, PA: Papers of the Eastern Chapter, Historical Society of the Evangelical and Reformed Church, 1964).

7. The material in the next few paragraphs is adapted from Douglas A. Sweeney, "'Falling Away from the General Faith of the Reformation'? The Contest over Calvinism in Nineteenth-Century America," in *John Calvin's American Legacy*, ed. Thomas J. Davis (New York: Oxford University Press, 2010), 111–46.

8. Edward Robinson, "Theological Education in Germany," *The Biblical Repository* 1 (January 1831): 1. For more on Robinson's importance as a conduit of German academic thought to America, see Thomas Albert Howard, "German Academic Theology in America: The Case of Edward Robinson and Philip Schaff," *History of Universities* 18, no. 1 (2003): 102–23.

had railed against it. Even the worldly Thomas Jefferson had warned against the allure of the effete cultures of Europe on the lives of young Americans who ought to be taught instead to search for *useful* knowledge and cultivate the virtues.[9]

During the early nineteenth century, the Napoleonic wars had kept most young people from Europe and its harmful new ideas. Some Americans, like Hodge, made it to Germany for study during the 1820s and '30s; others imbibed Germanic thought through various English-language channels such as Samuel Taylor Coleridge and Scotland's Thomas Carlyle.[10] Over the course of the next century, though, ten thousand Americans would study in German schools. By the late 1840s, they were doing so with alacrity, as if released at last to compensate for lost time.[11] Noah Porter depicted their pilgrimage in 1857:

> The impulse to go has for the last ten years gathered strength in a geometrical ratio, and is becoming almost a furore. Pastors leave their pulpits, professors their chairs, graduates rush from their Alma-Mater, undergraduates separate themselves from their college classes, that they may study in Germany, as though in Germany alone were the keys of knowledge; and as though from the very atmosphere of that favored land, a man must inhale the inspiration both of scholarship and genius.[12]

Many would continue to bemoan this German influence for generations to come. But many others embraced it. Porter himself encouraged

9. Jefferson wrote from Paris regarding the training of his nephew: "Of all the errors which can possibly be committed in the education of youth, that of sending them to Europe is the most fatal. I see [clearly] that no American should come to Europe under 30 years of age: and [he who] does, will lose in science, in virtue, in health and in happiness, for which manners are a poor compensation, were we even to admit the hollow, unmeaning manners of Europe to be preferable to the simplicity and sincerity of our own country." Thomas Jefferson to Walker Maury, August 19, 1785, in Julian P. Boyd, ed., *The Papers of Thomas Jefferson*, vol. 8, *25 February to 31 October 1785* (Princeton: Princeton University Press, 1953), 409–10.

10. On this phenomenon, see especially Noah Porter, "Coleridge and His American Disciples," *Bibliotheca Sacra* 4 (February 1847): 117–71; and Anson Phelps Stokes, *Memorials of Eminent Yale Men: A Biographical Study of Student Life and University Influences during the Eighteenth and Nineteenth Centuries*, vol. 1, *Religion and Letters* (New Haven: Yale University Press, 1914), 329–30.

11. For a brief but current account of this American migration, see Gary Dorrien, *The Making of American Liberal Theology: Imagining Progressive Religion, 1805–1900* (Louisville: Westminster John Knox, 2001), 403–4.

12. Noah Porter, "The American Student in Germany," *The New Englander* 15 (November 1857): 575.

Americans to cross the sea to Germany, but with their eyes wide open to the risks that were involved. "The theologians who are infected with the tendency to Germanize in the worst sense of the term," he said, "are those whose German studies are prosecuted at second hand and perhaps with little knowledge of the language."

> But let a student of a manly intellect and an honest faith go to Germany and hear for himself, and the charm if any with which error was invested at a distance will be likely to disappear on closer inspection. The heresy and falsehood which smelled like musk across the ocean emits the rank odor of putrefaction as he draws near. . . . The power to separate the truth from error is greatly enhanced, when the language is made familiar and unusual modes of thinking are mastered.[13]

As Nevin sought to straddle the cultural tensions of his age, his new German-American church, and his own spiritual journey, he acknowledged his debt to the Germans while insisting that he disavowed their modern liberal heresies. "I am a debtor . . . both to the English and the Germans," he explained, "both to Princeton and Berlin." He admired Friedrich Schleiermacher, but never aped his teaching. August Neander had changed Nevin's life by helping him think historically about the Christian faith. But even Neander, Nevin knew, relied too heavily on Schleiermacher and failed to guard sufficiently against romantic error. Still, Nevin could hardly understand why Anglo-centric critics wanted to throw the German baby out with the bathwater. He expressed his frank bewilderment in the introduction to Philip Schaff's *The Principle of Protestantism* (1845):

> Some . . . seem to have the idea that whatever is characteristically German must be theologically bad. . . . Now I would be sorry to appear as the apologist of either German philosophy or German theology as a whole. Few probably have been exercised with more solemn fears than myself, in this very direction. One thing however is most certain. The zeal affected by a large class of persons in this country against German thinking is not according to knowledge.[14]

Nevin's colleague Frederick Gast verified his sound discernment when it came to German views: "Certain thinkers," granted Gast,

13. Porter, "American Student in Germany," 588.
14. John W. Nevin, introduction to Philip Schaff, *The Principle of Protestantism,* trans. John W. Nevin (1845; Philadelphia: United Church Press, 1964), 30–32.

such as "Schleiermacher, Neander and Rothe possessed a wonderful fascination for him; but he never followed them blindly, or surrendered himself to them." In response to those who claimed he *had* surrendered to the Germans, Nevin balked and begged for empathy. "Am I not a teacher in the German church," he asked, "and as such bound, in common honesty, to cultivate a proper connection with the theological life of Germany, as well as with that of Scotland and New England?"[15] Nevin's familiarity with German scholarship, he suggested, was the duty of a man in his position within the denomination. But more important than his reasons was his legacy, for Nevin's familiarity with German thought would contribute to a new era of christological reflection in America.

The Rise of American Christocentrism

Nevin's role as a teacher in the German Reformed Church had led him to ask questions, develop themes, and explore sources that other Anglophone Americans had yet to consider carefully. His students looked to Heidelberg for doctrinal orientation.[16] Their churches worshiped somewhat more liturgically than most of those attended by their neighbors.[17] And church members had a facility with German language and literature uncommon in the mainstream of American Christianity. But what did all this mean for the development of Christology?

It meant that Nevin was well-positioned to mediate between the latest trends in German thought, the concerns of the clergy in the German Reformed Church, and the idiosyncrasies of American Christianity. And it meant that insofar as German scholars were converging on the study of Christology, he would translate their scholarship

15. Frederick A. Gast, introduction to Appel, *Life and Work of John Williamson Nevin*, vii; and Nevin, *My Own Life*, 96–127, 139–49; John W. Nevin, *Antichrist; or the Spirit of Sect and Schism* (New York: John S. Taylor, 1848), 3–4, 17.

16. The German Reformed Church subscribed to the Heidelberg Catechism, compiled in 1562 as a standard for the churches of the Palatinate. See *The Heidelberg Catechism*, in *The Creeds of Christendom, with a History and Critical Notes*, ed. Philip Schaff (Grand Rapids: Baker Books, 1996), 3:307–55.

17. Liturgical matters were contested in the German Reformed Church, however, as high-church followers of the Mercersburg Theology were criticized by many of the clergy. For helpful summaries of this contest, see Jack Martin Maxwell, *Worship and Reformed Theology: The Liturgical Lessons of Mercersburg*, Pittsburgh Theological Monograph Series (Pittsburgh: Pickwick Press, 1976); and Hart, *John Williamson Nevin*, 197–223.

for Christians in America. In the process, he moved away from the churches of his youth (especially churches under the spell of Charles Finney's "new measures," which Nevin castigated famously in his best-known book).[18] But as he did so, he called his fellow Americans to follow him, reminding them of their catholic faith and their Reformation heritage, and pointing leading thinkers to a deeper ecclesiology than most had ever known. He did not develop a fully orbed, compassionate Christology. But he did develop a christocentric vision of the church, and the church's role in the world, that moved the incarnation of God to center stage in the drama of American theology during a time when this was quite a controversial thing to do. As Nevin himself would recollect in 1882,

> Less than half a century ago . . . the very terms Christological and Christocentric . . . were viewed by many with grave apprehension and distrust. Did they not carry with them an echo of Schleiermacher? Had they not in them a touch of Hegelian pantheism? At any rate, could they not be felt to be somehow off the track of modern evangelicalism, not harmonizing rightly with its pet traditional shibboleths . . . ? Be the case as it might, the system which pretended to make full earnest with the idea that Jesus Christ is himself literally the entire sum and substance of Christianity, was not in favor with our American churches generally. . . . But all that, it appears, is now past. The era of Christological theology has set in with a force which may be said, so far at least as profession goes, to carry all before it. Our evangelical denominations are in a sort of haste to put themselves right in regard to this point. The significance of Christ's person is paraded on every hand, as the only true centre of Christianity, as the only real soul of a living Christian faith.[19]

Nevin pioneered this christological development. While his most important book, *The Mystical Presence* (1846), dealt with the Eucharist, it interpreted the sacrament by stressing its metaphysical and

---

18. On the Finneyites and their measures, see Charles E. Hambrick-Stowe, *Charles G. Finney and the Spirit of American Evangelicalism*, Library of Religious Biography (Grand Rapids: Eerdmans, 1996); Keith J. Hardman, *Charles Grandison Finney, 1792–1875: Revivalist and Reformer* (Syracuse: Syracuse University Press, 1987); and the helpful bibliography in Garth M. Rosell and Richard A. G. Dupuis, eds., *The Memoirs of Charles G. Finney: The Complete Restored Text* (Grand Rapids: Zondervan, 1989), 671–701. For more on Nevin's opposition to them, see John W. Nevin, *The Anxious Bench* (Chambersburg, PA: Printed at the office of the *Weekly Messenger*, 1843; rev. ed., 1844).

19. John W. Nevin, "Christ the Inspiration of His Own Word," *Reformed Quarterly Review* 29 (January 1882): 5–6.

christological substance. Beginning with this volume, he portrayed the incarnation as "the principle," the "true measure and test" of "Christianity," decentering the Anglo-Protestant emphasis on sin and true conversion as the core of Christian faith. He described the incarnation as "the fact of all facts," the "centre and hinge of all history."[20] In accordance with a current then pulsating in Germany, he suggested that the incarnation might have taken place without the fall of Adam and Eve.[21] And then in keeping with a historic catholic theological tendency (identified most famously with the work of Irenaeus), Nevin suggested that God intended the incarnation not primarily for the sake of the atonement—though the atonement was essential—but to recapitulate his ultimate, prelapsarian end (or goal) of creation: to crown the human race with genuine fellowship with God, raising us up to dwell with him in perfect love for all eternity. Or, as Nevin often phrased this, "The Word became flesh . . . for the purpose not simply of effecting a salvation that might become available for men in an outward way, but to open a fountain of life in our nature itself,

20. John W. Nevin, *The Mystical Presence: A Vindication of the Reformed or Calvinistic Doctrine of the Holy Eucharist* (Philadelphia: J. B. Lippincott, 1846), 5, 209; and John W. Nevin, "Liebner's Christology," *Mercersburg Review* 3 (January 1851): 70.

21. Nevin wondered about, and waffled on, this question throughout his life. When reviewing the works of scholars such as Theodor Albert Liebner, who taught that the incarnation would have happened even without the fall, Nevin seemed to offer consent. But then when writing about the critique of Liebner's doctrine by Julius Müller (published as two articles in the *Deutsche Zeitschrift für christliche Wissenschaft und christliches Leben*, ed. Karl F. T. Schneider [Berlin: Wiegandt und Grieben, 1850]), Nevin appeared to be less certain and to side with Müller instead. Compare Nevin, "Liebner's Christology," with John W. Nevin, "Cur Deus Homo?" *Mercersburg Review* 3 (May 1851): 220–38 (Nevin's article on Müller). Even later in life, Nevin wondered if Liebner was correct. See John W. Nevin, "The Revelation of God in Christ," *Mercersburg Review* 18 (July 1871): 325–42, in which he wrote the following: "Whether the Divine Logos would not have become incarnate even if sin had not entered into the world, is a still wider question, in regard to which as we know there is room for a difference of opinion. There is much certainly which seems to favor such a thought; although we must admit that it lies beyond the horizon of the evangelical revelation, and it is best therefore, perhaps, to bow before it with reverential silence" (325). The best secondary source on this confusion in Nevin's corpus is Nichols, *Romanticism in American Theology*, 146–50. But Nichols thought that Nevin's fascination with this question came to an end when he read Müller. For a helpful recent analysis of the doctrinal issues at stake, see Edwin Chr. Van Driel, *Incarnation Anyway: Arguments for Supralapsarian Christology*, Academy Series (New York: Oxford University Press, 2008), who treats the notion that the incarnation would have occurred without the fall as found in Schleiermacher, Isaak Dorner, and Karl Barth.

that might thenceforward continue to flow over to other men, as a vivific stream, to the end of time."[22] In this way, Nevin gave special attention to the life of Christ between his virgin birth and resurrection. Christ came not just to die but, significantly, to live. That life puts him in intimate communion with believers today.

In short, for Nevin the incarnation was the apex of creation, the source of our redemption, and the basis of our real, intimate union with the Lord. As he wrote in *The Mystical Presence*, "the object of the incarnation was to couple the human nature in real union with the Logos, as a permanent source of life." God assumed our human nature, not only to save us from our sin, but also to enfold us in his love, raising us up to a new and higher spiritual form of life. Those united to Christ by faith, then, "are incorporated into his very nature," Nevin insisted, "and made to subsist with him." Or, as he preached before Communion at a Reformed Church convention, there is "an actual union between Christ and his people, mystical but in the highest sense real, in virtue of which they are as closely joined to him, as the limbs are to the head in the natural body. They are in him, and he is in them, not figuratively but truly." The "end of . . . Christianity," Nevin declaimed constantly, "is living fellowship and communion with God" in Christ.[23]

This emphasis on union meant that God has come quite near to us and is drawing us near to himself. He is not the distant Father frequently caricatured by critics of Nevin's Calvinistic faith. In fact, Nevin went so far at times as to say that Christ assumed not only a single human nature, but humanity in general, and "transfused" it "with the inmost essence of the divine." He was not a universalist. But he did maintain an Irenaean view of Jesus's role as humanity's "second Adam," who accomplishes in us what Adam and Eve failed to

22. Nevin, *Mystical Presence*, 68. Calvin himself had this Irenaean quality, as demonstrated in Julie Canlis's helpful book, *Calvin's Ladder: A Spiritual Theology of Ascent and Ascension* (Grand Rapids: Eerdmans, 2010). Canlis offers an intriguing comparison of Calvin and Irenaeus on the ways in which Christ recapitulates God's original intentions for humanity, elevating us by his Spirit toward ever more intimate fellowship with God.

23. Nevin, *Mystical Presence*, 165, 54, 122; and John W. Nevin, "Undying Life in Christ," in Appel, *Life and Work of John Williamson Nevin*, 626. Though Nevin tended to present his strong emphasis on the doctrine of the *unio cum christo* as a correction to the "Puritan" thought of most of his interlocutors, it actually had a long (though less "mystical") history in early modern Reformed thought. See Richard A. Muller, *Calvin and the Reformed Tradition: On the Work of Christ and the Order of Salvation* (Grand Rapids: Baker Academic, 2012), 202–43.

accomplish when they alienated the race from the loving presence of God. Jesus made us near to God especially by suffering for our sin, he said, and in this way still makes us near to God today. His incarnation "called the Saviour to suffer" with us, Nevin wrote, which tempers the triumphalism of other Western christologies by highlighting the grief more than the victory of Christ: "As the bearer of a fallen humanity he must descend with it to the lowest depths of sorrow and pain, in order that he might triumph with it again in the power of his own imperishable life." Our communion with his life has been enabled by his passion, which was far more intense than any merely human suffering—and demonstrates that God empathizes with the oppressed. Nevin noted in evident wonder that the Bible provides only glimpses

> of the general opening of the kingdom of heaven through the travail of Christ's soul, in his weary journey from the womb of the virgin to his death on the cross. These glimpses . . . must be regarded always as only dimly representing what he was called to encounter in his inward spiritual life; while in the nature of the case the actual experiences of that life altogether must infinitely transcend all that can enter intelligibly the highest thought either of men or of angels. . . . What is said of [Jesus's] sufferings in Gethsemane—the exceeding sorrow, the agony, the bloody sweat—is only a transient unexaggerated picture of what his inward life was all along; the "man of sorrows and acquainted with grief" (Is. liii).

Jesus's suffering, both in body and in spirit, demonstrated the profundity of his solidarity with us in our pain. Moreover, Nevin insisted that Christ maintained this solidarity with humankind eternally; his glorious resurrection did not diminish it. Christ's triumph over the grave does not suggest, in Nevin's thought, that God is now far removed from human life and human pain. "In dying, and rising again from the dead," Nevin affirmed, Jesus did "[pass] into a new order of existence." But this "amounted in no sense to a sundering of himself, from the life of the human world. . . . His resurrection," rather, "served . . . to bring him more intimately and deeply into the heart of this life, and to make him in this way the principle of redemption for it more powerfully and efficaciously than before."[24]

24. Nevin, "Christ the Inspiration of His Own Word," 26, 24; Nevin, *Mystical Presence*, 166; and J. W. Nevin, "Once for All," *Mercersburg Review* 17 (January 1870): 112. For more of Nevin's Christology and incarnational thinking, see esp.

Nevin was a privileged man, a powerful academic. He never found himself as far along the *Via Dolorosa* as some of the others we will discuss in later chapters. Nor did he formulate the kind of detailed christological doctrine found in the work of other systematic theologians. Nevin's suffering, in the main, was psychological and spiritual—like the suffering of most privileged, white, Western academics (the two of us included). He spent the bulk of his time reflecting on matters other than Christology. But he pioneered a shift in American theological history from revival to the church, from conversion to sanctification, from British to German frames of reference, from expiation to incarnation. Not all would follow his lead. And those who did experienced theological gains as well as losses.[25] But the gains included a way of speaking of God that rendered him near, in the person and work of Christ, for salvation and, more importantly, for the union of the church with God himself. Nevin assured all those who heard him and believed in Jesus Christ that the Lord was not aloof. Rather, God was with them constantly, passionately, intimately. Christ had suffered and died to draw them into the life of God, both now and for eternity.

John W. Nevin, "The Trinitarian and Unitarian Doctrines Concerning Jesus Christ," *The Presbyterian Preacher* 1 (October 1832): 65–80; John W. Nevin, "Sartorius on the Person and Work of Christ," *Mercersburg Review* 1 (March 1849): 146–64, a review of Ernst Sartorius (general superintendent and consistorial director at Koenigsberg, Prussia), *Die Lehre von Christi Person und Werk in populairen Vorlesungen vorgetragen*, 5th ed. (Hamburg: Friedrich Perthes, 1845), as well as the English translation of this work by Oakman Stearns, *The Person and Work of Christ* (Boston: Gould, Kendall, & Lincoln, 1848), which Nevin thought was terrible; John W. Nevin, "Wilberforce on the Incarnation," *Mercersburg Review* 2 (March 1850): 164–96, a review of Robert Isaac Wilberforce (Archdeacon of the East Riding), *The Doctrine of the Incarnation of our Lord Jesus Christ in Its Relation to Mankind and to the Church*, 1st American ed. from the 2nd London ed. (Philadelphia: H. Hooker, 1849), which Nevin liked but found too snootily Anglocentric; John W. Nevin, "Jesus and the Resurrection," *Mercersburg Review* 13 (April 1861): 169–90; John W. Nevin, *Christ, and Him Crucified: A Concio ad Clerum, Preached in Grace Church, Pittsburgh, November 18, 1863, at the Opening of the First General Synod of the German Reformed Church in America* (Pittsburgh: J. McMillin, 1863); and John W. Nevin, "The Testimony of Jesus," *Mercersburg Review* 24 (January 1877): 5–33.

25. They risked substituting the vagaries of transcendental thinking for a Protestant understanding of God's supernatural grace imputed forensically to undeserving sinners. Their Calvinist opponents said that God saves sinners with their Savior's alien righteousness—not the risen life of Christ conveyed organically by means of history, church, and sacraments. For more on their engagement with opponents on these matters, see Sweeney, "'Falling Away from the General Faith of the Reformation'?" 113–25.

2

Franz Pieper
and the Suffering of God

If John Williamson Nevin moved us closer to the compassionate
Christology we seek with his emphasis on the *incarnation* of God
in Jesus Christ, Franz Pieper (1852–1931) nearly conceptualized it for
us with his doctrine of the *suffering* of God in the person of Christ.
Pieper's world, like that of Nevin, was traditional and German—
rooted deeply in the soil of the Lutheran Reformation and concerned
about the desiccation of robust catholic doctrine in the heat of the
Enlightenment. Unlike Nevin, though, Pieper lacked roots in modern
America and its national social history. And this helps us understand
both why his doctrine is compelling for our christological purposes and
why most other Christians have ignored it. Whereas Nevin *recontex-*
tualized the doctrine of the believer's union with God through Christ
and the church by means of nineteenth-century language and with
his evangelical neighbors at the forefront of his mind, Pieper sought
to *reiterate* the doctrine of the passion of God in Christ using the
language of the Lutheran Reformation. That is, Pieper never served as
a mediating figure (like Nevin clearly had), working to bridge the gap
between his own tradition and the lives of those around him. In fact,
he surely would have refused to play that role if he had been asked.
We nonetheless conscript him into this role for present purposes.

We dare think he approves from his now-glorified and much more ecumenical point of view.

Pieper was an immigrant who lived the bulk of his life within an ingrown German church. Raised in Prussia, he moved at the age of eighteen to America, where he attended German schools and pastored German Lutheran churches. He went on to serve on the faculty of Concordia Seminary (St. Louis, Missouri), led the school as president (1887–1931), and even directed its Germanic Lutheran Church–Missouri Synod as denominational president (1899–1911) as well. His cultural distance from his adopted land engendered shrewd reflection on the weaknesses of mainstream American theology and makes him a useful resource in our study of Christology. As noted above, however, this cultural distance also explains his near obscurity beyond the bounds of Lutheran orthodoxy. His conservatism is often dismissed as "fundamentalism" even by modern American Lutherans (who are more at home in their surroundings and with modern Western liberalism than Pieper ever was). His keen sense of German identity and clumsiness in English render him foreign to Anglophone and other non-Teutonic readers. And his denomination's inwardness and deep-seated concern about the state of other Christians have kept it from making much of a difference in the larger Christian world. Its Christology, however, represented best by Pieper, has potential to speak powerfully to those of us who seek a warmer view of God in Christ.[1]

---

1. What little scholarship there is on Pieper's thought is sharply divided and is written by insiders who are struggling for control of American Lutheranism. Some interpret Pieper as an intransigent fundamentalist, others as a champion of the faith in troubled times. The former include Leigh D. Jordahl, "The Theology of Franz Pieper: A Resource for Fundamentalistic Thought Modes among American Lutherans," *Lutheran Quarterly* 23 (May 1971): 118–37; Richard E. Koenig, "What's Behind the Showdown in the LCMS? Church and Tradition in Collision," *Lutheran Forum* 6 (November 1972): 17–20; Koenig, "What's Behind the Showdown in the LCMS? Missouri Turns Moderate: 1938–65," *Lutheran Forum* 7 (February 1973): 19–20, 29; Koenig, "What's Behind the Showdown in the LCMS? Conservative Reaction: 1965–69," *Lutheran Forum* 7 (May 1973): 18–21; and Mary Todd, *Authority Vested: A Story of Identity and Change in the Lutheran Church–Missouri Synod* (Grand Rapids: Eerdmans, 2000), 98–99, 140–41. The latter include Theodore Graebner, *Dr. Francis Pieper: A Biographical Sketch* (St. Louis: Concordia, 1931); Frederick Photenhauer, "Funeral Sermon for Dr. Pieper," trans. M. C. Harrison, *Concordia Historical Institute Quarterly* 66 (Spring 1993): 39–42; and David P. Scaer, "Francis Pieper," in *Handbook of Evangelical Theologians*, ed. Walter A. Elwell (Grand Rapids: Baker Books, 1993), 40–53 (the most even-handed treatment of Pieper available).

As we will state more fully below, Pieper's contribution is this: he enables us to complement the American *Christus victor* with a tender and compassionate American *Christus dolor* without abandoning the doctrine of divine impassibility, which has long been central to most Christian views of God. He offers a way of speaking technically of God's vulnerability in the person of Jesus Christ—pointing clearly and reliably to real divine passion—without rendering God himself subject to suffering and pain; that is, without depicting God himself as "passible," as many of our contemporaries do. The notion of God's impassibility is central to what many label "classical theism." First formulated by Aristotle and other ancient Greeks, it was also taught by the early church fathers from the Bible (Ps. 102:25–27; Rom. 1:23; 1 Tim. 6:15–16; Heb. 1:10–12; James 1:17; etc.) and became a key part of their official doctrine of God. For Pieper, as for most other Christians in his day, it was a nonnegotiable tenet of traditional Christian faith. Because few in his world disputed it, he rarely thematized it or defended it explicitly.[2] But it lurked in the background of his christological writings, placing limits on his statements about the suffering of God and making Pieper an unusually helpful benchmark for believers who want to preserve doctrinal orthodoxy without embracing the notion of a distant, cold, and apathetic God.[3]

2. He did do so occasionally, as in Francis Pieper, *Christian Dogmatics* (St. Louis: Concordia, 1950), 2:139–41, 233–35, 253, from which we will quote below. The English edition of Pieper's *Dogmatics* is based on Franz Pieper, *Christliche Dogmatik*, 3 vols. (St. Louis: Concordia, 1917–1924). Walter W. F. Albrecht added the fourth index volume to the English-language edition in 1957.

3. Aristotle's (now infamous) "apathy axiom," in which the unmoved mover who exists "of necessity" is by definition "impassible," may be found in his *Metaphysics* 12.7 (English trans. in Richard McKeon, ed., *Introduction to Aristotle*, 2nd ed. [1947; Chicago: University of Chicago Press, 1973], 318–20). For an up-to-date reflection of the state of the conversation among Christians on this doctrine, see James F. Keating and Thomas Joseph White, eds., *Divine Impassibility and the Mystery of Human Suffering* (Grand Rapids: Eerdmans, 2009). For an excellent defense of a traditional Roman Catholic understanding of the doctrine, see Thomas G. Weinandy, *Does God Suffer?* (Notre Dame: University of Notre Dame Press, 2000), but note Weinandy's concern to guard his christological language in opposition to Luther, Calvin, and their liberal Protestant heirs. John Kenneth Mozley, *The Impassibility of God: A Survey of Christian Thought* (Cambridge: Cambridge University Press, 1926), remains a classic, helpful survey of the early movement away from divine impassibility by liberal Protestant thinkers. For the best recent attempt to do justice to the church fathers' view of divine impassibility, which was qualified by their notion that God is fully involved in the world, that he suffered in Jesus Christ, and that this doctrine is problematic (though reliable and true), see Paul L. Gavrilyuk, *The Suffering of the*

Pieper made this contribution using premodern language and scholastic terminology, distinguishing between what we can say of God in Christ (*in concreto*, in the flesh) and what we can say of God himself (or of the Godhead in itself) considered apart from Jesus Christ (*in abstracto*, as it were). This academic terminology gave Pieper special tools with which to fashion his Christology. But it makes some people nervous—especially the Reformed. Some worry that by saying *God* was vulnerable in Christ, that he suffered much as we do, Pieper verged on domesticating our understanding of God, undermining his transcendence or his infinite and qualitative distinction from humanity. Others complain that Pieper's doctrine harbors an inconsistency, for how could God both suffer in Christ and yet remain impassible? We offer his teaching, then, not as an incontestable monument to Protestant orthodoxy (as some of his followers do), nor as the be-all and end-all of our christological journey, but as a resource for honoring the fears of friends in Japan—and many other places, too—about the dangers of a Western or American *Christus victor* insufficiently acquainted with infirmity (cf. Isa. 53:3). We present it as a way of speaking of God's real compassion, empathetic love, and care, without transgressing the classical bounds of Christian orthodoxy.

Christus Dolor in the Lutheran Tradition

Pieper viewed his emphasis on the suffering of God as an inheritance from Scripture and tradition. As a conservative, confessional, dogmatic theologian, he positioned himself deliberately in a long and hallowed line of Lutheran christological teaching that accentuated the passion of God in Christ. He understood the challenges inherent in the task of teaching both that God is impassible and that God has truly suffered in the person of Jesus of Nazareth. But Pieper sinned boldly, claiming both of these things at once in the company of the saints (or his favorite saints, at least). He did so mainly from the Bible, of course, but he also appealed to the ancient church, Luther, Martin Chemnitz, and the Lutheran *Book of Concord* (1580)—not to mention the scholastic Lutheran writers near at hand.[4]

Impassible God: The Dialectics of Patristic Thought, Oxford Early Christian Studies (Oxford: Oxford University Press, 2004).

4. As evidence of Pieper's struggle to reconcile these seemingly inconsistent biblical truths, see his *Christian Dogmatics*, 2:139–41, 253.

Luther himself was hardly shy about discussing the suffering of God. Throughout his exegetical writings he affirmed what he believed the Scriptures teach about the passion of the Word of God made flesh (John 1), "the Lord of glory" who was "crucified" (1 Cor. 2:8), "the image of the invisible God" (Col. 1:15), the One in whom "the whole fullness of deity dwells bodily" (Col. 2:9), *das Ebenbild* or "imprint" of God's very being perfected through suffering (Heb. 1:3; 2:10). His best known comment on divine vulnerability in Christ comes from a sermon on John 4, in which he said at verse two that Christ's "two natures are so united . . . that Mary suckles God with her breasts, bathes God, rocks him, and carries him; furthermore, that Pilate and Herod crucified and killed God."[5]

This striking doctrine had been codified in Luther's earlier treatise *On the Councils and the Church* (1539), in which he claimed that "if it cannot be said that God died for us, but only a man, we are lost; but if God's death and a dead God lie in the balance, his side goes down and ours goes up like a light and empty scale." The incarnation of God proved crucial to Luther's thought, just as it later would for Nevin, who claimed Luther as an authority. Luther exceeded Nevin, though, and other Reformed thinkers too, by stating boldly (some say bluntly) that God suffered and died in Christ and that the death of God was necessary to rescue us from sin. It was precisely this claim, in fact, that made the incarnation crucial to Luther's whole theology—and also problematic. For while the death of God was necessary, it was inconceivable. God "could not sit on the scale unless he had become a man like us, so that it could be called God's dying, God's martyrdom, God's blood, and God's death." But God's death is utter foolishness, an unapproachable mystery (1 Cor. 1–2): "For God in his own nature cannot die; but now that God and man are united in one person, it is called God's death when the man dies who is one substance or one person with God."[6]

5. Martin Luther, *Sermons on the Gospel of St. John: Chapters 1–4*, in *Luther's Works* (henceforth, *LW*), vol. 22, ed. Jaroslav Pelikan (St. Louis: Concordia, 1957), 491–93. For the original German (1540), see the *Weimar-Ausgabe* edition of his works (henceforth, *WA*), 47:199–200.

6. Martin Luther, *On the Councils and the Church*, in *LW*, vol. 41, ed. Eric W. Gritsch (Philadelphia: Fortress, 1966), 103–4 (*WA*, 50:589–90). Luther discusses the suffering and death of God in Christ in other places, including *LW*, 24:106–7 (*WA*, 45:557–58); *LW*, 37:210–11 (*WA*, 26:321–22); and his *Disputatio de divinitate et humanitate Christi* (1540), available in *WA*, 39/II:92–121 (see esp. thesis #4), but not in *LW*. (Christopher B. Brown offers an English translation at *Project Wittenberg*: http://www.iclnet.org/pub/

Later Lutheran theologians cited this formulation frequently, interpreting it in light of ancient statements concerning God as well as the person of Jesus Christ. They also furthered its assertion about the suffering of God by means of the ancient Christian doctrine of the "communication of properties," or idioms, in Christ (*communicatio idiomatum*), which regulated statements about cooperation between the Lord's divine and human natures.[7] They remained within the bounds of the Definition of Chalcedon (451) and "acknowledged," in the famous words of the Definition itself, that Christ's "two natures . . . undergo no confusion, no change, no division, no separation." The Lord's natures remain distinct, even as they interact cooperatively for us and our salvation, as the Definition of Chalcedon states:

> At no point was the difference between the natures taken away through the union, but rather the property of both natures is preserved and comes together into a single person and a single subsistent being; he is not parted or divided into two persons, but is one and the same only-begotten Son, God, Word, Lord Jesus Christ, just as the prophets taught from the beginning about him, and as the Lord Jesus Christ himself instructed us, and as the creed of the fathers handed it down to us.[8]

---

resources/text/wittenberg/luther/luther-divinity.txt.) Dennis Ngien has also written rather extensively on this subject with an eye on recent debates about divine impassibility. He radicalizes Luther's sometimes inconsistent statements about the communication of divine and human properties in Christ, thereby (falsely) rendering Luther as a source of the late-modern affirmation of divine passibility. See esp. Dennis Ngien, *The Suffering of God According to Martin Luther's 'Theologia Crucis,'* American University Studies (New York: Peter Lang, 1995); Dennis Ngien, "Chalcedonian Christology and Beyond: Luther's Understanding of the *Communicatio Idiomatum*," *Heythrop Journal* 45 (2004): 54–68; and Dennis Ngien, "Ultimate Reality and Meaning in Luther's Theology of the Cross: No Other God but the Incarnate God," *Andrews University Seminary Studies* 42 (2004): 383–405. An erudite correction of Ngien (among several others who commit the same mistake) may be found in David J. Luy, "Dominus Mortis: Martin Luther on the Incorruptibility of God in Christ" (Ph.D. diss., Marquette University, 2012). Luther's theology of the cross suffuses his christological writings. An excellent English-language introduction may be found in Robert Kolb, "Luther on the Theology of the Cross," *Lutheran Quarterly* 16 (Winter 2002): 443–66.

7. For a concise definition of the *communicatio idiomatum* according to early Protestant thinkers, see Richard A. Muller, *Dictionary of Latin and Greek Theological Terms: Drawn Principally from Protestant Scholastic Theology* (Grand Rapids: Baker Books, 1985), 72–74.

8. We have followed the English translation in *Decrees of the Ecumenical Councils*, vol. 1, *Nicaea I to Lateran V*, ed. Norman P. Tanner (London: Sheed & Ward, 1990), 86–87.

But they also honored the boundaries of the Council of Ephesus (431), which was called to combat Nestorianism and safeguarded the *unity* of Jesus's personality in even stronger terms than those of Chalcedon: "we confess one Christ," it said, "one Son, one Lord . . . we confess the holy virgin to be the mother of God because God the Word took flesh and became man and from his very conception united to himself the temple he took from her."[9] They maintained, furthermore, with several early church fathers, especially John of Damascus, that the human nature of Jesus Christ is "enhypostatic"—it subsists not in itself but in the person of the Word and therefore shares in his divine characteristics.[10]

These early Lutherans insisted that the communication of properties, or idioms, in Christ is only a top-down affair. While the human nature of Jesus shares the Lord's divine properties, his human characteristics are not transferred up to God. Still, they argued forcefully—much more forcefully than most—that Christ's divinity and majesty are shared by his humanity. When he suffered and died as a man, then, God suffered with him. Or as stated in Article VIII of the *Formula of Concord* (1577):

> Because of [the] personal union, without which this kind of true communion of the natures is unthinkable and impossible, not only the bare human nature (which possesses the characteristics of suffering and dying) suffered for the sins of the entire world, but the Son of God himself suffered (according to the assumed human nature) and, according to our simple Christian creed, truly died—although the divine nature can neither suffer nor die.

This definitive confessional declaration went even further:

> We hold and teach with the ancient, orthodox church, as it explained this teaching on the basis of Scripture, that the human nature in Christ has received this majesty according to the mode of the personal union, namely, because "the whole fullness of deity" [Col. 2:9] dwells in Christ, not as in other godly people or angels, but "bodily" as in its own body. This fullness, with all its majesty, power, glory, and efficacy, spontaneously shines forth in the assumed human nature when and how Christ wishes. . . . We regard it as a harmful error to remove this majesty from Christ according to his humanity. This deprives Christians of their highest

9. Tanner, *Decrees of the Ecumenical Councils*, 1:70.
10. See Muller, *Dictionary of Latin and Greek Theological Terms*, 35, 103.

comfort, which they have in the promise he gave them—the promise of the presence and indwelling of their head, king, and high priest. He promised them that not only his naked deity, which for us sinners is like a consuming fire on dried-up stubble [cf. Exod. 15:7], would be with them. He also promised that he would be present—he, the human being who had spoken with them, who had experienced every tribulation in the assumed human nature, who for this reason can have sympathy with us as fellow human beings; he wants to be with us in all our troubles.[11]

The human nature of Jesus is invested with divinity and sympathizes with us in our earthly tribulations. This is the wonder and the blessing of the incarnation of God. God is really with us now—in Christ, and in the concrete means of his presence in the church—even amid our worldly sorrow and distress.

Martin Chemnitz stood behind this formulation of the matter. A leading figure in the debates among the sixteenth-century Lutherans that culminated in the famous *Formula of Concord*, he was second only to Luther as an authority for Pieper and Missouri Synod Lutherans. Chemnitz's treatise on *The Two Natures in Christ* (1578) appeared the following year.[12] This treatise and the *Formula* were buttressed, furthermore, by the little-known but highly influential list of statements by the early church fathers called the "Catalog of Testimonies," organized by Chemnitz and his colleague Jakob Andreae and printed with the *Formula* in many early editions, showing support for their Christology from doctors of the church.[13] Lutheran theologians had several precedents, both in the early church and in the more recent Lutheran tradition, for describing the suffering of God in Christ.

11. Article VIII of the *Formula of Concord* (Solid Declaration), published in 1577, as presented in *The Book of Concord: The Confessions of the Evangelical Lutheran Church*, ed. Robert Kolb and Timothy J. Wengert (Minneapolis: Fortress, 2000), 616–34 (quotations from 619, 628, 633).

12. Martin Chemnitz, *The Two Natures in Christ*, trans. J. A. O. Preus (St. Louis: Concordia, 1971), published in definitive form in Latin as *De Duabus Naturis in Christo* (Leipzig: Johannes Rhamba, 1578). Chemnitz (1522–86) pastored in Braunschweig. Andreae (1528–90) pastored in Württemberg and taught in Tübingen. For the teaching of other Lutheran scholastic thinkers on this doctrine, see Heinrich Schmid, *The Doctrinal Theology of the Evangelical Lutheran Church*, 3rd ed., trans. Charles A. Hay and Henry E. Jacobs (Minneapolis: Augsburg, 1899), 294–337, based on Schmid's *Dogmatik der Evangelisch Lutherischen Kirche* (Frankfurt: Heyder & Zimmer, 1863).

13. "Catalog of Testimonies," trans. Thomas Manteufel, in *Sources and Contexts of the Book of Concord*, ed. Robert Kolb and James A. Nestingen (Minneapolis: Fortress, 2001), 220–44.

Pieper on the Suffering of God in Christ

Pieper was not an innovator. He always considered himself to be a doctrinal "repristinator." His goal, he said, was to pass along the Scripture teaching synthesized best—once and for all—during the Lutheran Reformation.[14] He was a student of C. P. Krauth, the great defender of Lutheran orthodoxy in nineteenth-century America.[15] Like Krauth, he did respond to modern critics of his views. But he refused to revise his doctrine (or refused to admit revising it) in response to modern trends. Instead he worried, like Nevin, but to a much greater degree, that far too much Christian revision, indeed doctrinal attrition, had occurred in the modern West, which had allowed the church to drift away from its Reformation moorings. He repudiated the call to recontextualize his heritage in terms provided for him by his late-modern peers. Rather, he sought to rearticulate, as faithfully as possible, the Bible doctrine taught in the *Book of Concord*.

Therefore, Pieper taught the doctrine of Christ's suffering he had inherited.[16] He taught it from the Scriptures and the Lutheran confessions. He claimed that it had been "known and believed in Christendom from the very beginning, before any council passed any resolution," by everyone who kept the clear teaching of the Word.[17] Still, he followed Luther, Chemnitz, and the *Formula of Concord* as he systematized the doctrine, distinguishing his Lutheran view from that of other Christians, especially the Reformed, at every turn.[18]

He did so in a manner that is difficult for modern evangelicals to follow, unaccustomed as we are to old scholastic terminology. But Pieper's doctrine pivots on his use of that very language. So does his crucial contribution to our *Christus dolor* emphasis—so please stick with us as we summarize it briefly.

In keeping with tradition, he taught the impersonality (*anhypostasia*) of the human nature of Jesus. He denied that it subsisted in itself—that is, on its own, apart from the Word or Son of God. "While

14. Pieper defended this method at length in *Christian Dogmatics*, 1:ix–x, 149–86.

15. For Krauth's Christology, see Charles P. Krauth, *The Conservative Reformation and Its Theology: As Represented in the Augsburg Confession, and in the History and Literature of the Evangelical Lutheran Church* (Philadelphia: General Council Publication Board, 1871), 456–517.

16. Pieper's massive section on "The Doctrine of Christ (Christologia)" is found in *Christian Dogmatics*, 2:55–394.

17. Ibid., 57.

18. Pieper offered a "Summary Critique of Reformed Christology" in ibid., 271–79.

every other human nature also is a separate person," he wrote, "the human nature of Christ was received into the Person of the Son of God from the moment of its existence." It was enhypostatic (*enhypostasia*). It subsisted in, and only in, the eternal Son of God and thus, again, shared divine characteristics.[19]

He followed Chemnitz on the "communication of properties" in Christ, rehearsing at length the three *genera*, or three "kinds" (*genera* is the plural form of the Latin word *genus*, meaning "class," "group," or "kind"), of communication found in Chemnitz's magnum opus, under which this ancient doctrine had been taught by most Lutherans. There was the *genus idiomaticum*, or idiomatic kind, in which the attributes of Christ, "belonging essentially to only one nature, are always ascribed to the whole person, but the divine attributes according to the divine nature, and the human attributes according to the human nature." This echoed the ancient claim that Christ's two natures, while distinct, fueled the unified work of his entire personality. There was the *genus maiestaticum*, or genus of the majesty and glory of Jesus Christ, in which "the communication of divine properties to the human nature is . . . taught." This was the notion of the top-down sharing of divinity with Jesus's human nature. And finally, there was the *genus apotelesmaticum*, or the genus of accomplishment, in which "all official acts which Christ as Prophet, Priest, and King has performed and still performs for the salvation of men, he performs according to both natures, by each nature doing what is proper to it, not by itself and apart from the other nature, but in constant communion with the other, in one undivided theanthropic action." This affirmed the absolute cooperation of his natures, even on the cross.[20]

It was the *genus maiestaticum* that caused the most trouble, especially with the Reformed, and distinguished Pieper's Lutheran Christology. For it was the *genus maiestaticum* that made Jesus out to be a man in whom God suffered, died, and offers himself today—in finite form—through the ministries of Word and sacrament. Reformed thinkers tended to view the natures of Christ as more distinct, suggesting that sometimes he operated mainly from his divinity (as when performing miracles) while at other times he operated mainly from his humanity (as when dying on the cross). They felt that Pieper's

19. Ibid., 79–85 (quotation from 79).
20. Ibid., 132–279 (quotations from 143, 157, 247). Chemnitz laid out these three *genera* in *The Two Natures in Christ*, 161–68 (and passim), focusing on the *genus maiestaticum* on pp. 241–46.

Lutheran formula confused Jesus's natures, making it difficult to distinguish them in anything but theory and calling to mind the ancient heresy of the Monophysites.[21] "The finite is incapable of the infinite" (*finitum non capax infiniti*), they cried, in a slogan used frequently by anti-Lutheran Calvinists to drive home the point that finite things cannot receive, contain, or comprehend God.

Neither Pieper nor his authorities had ever claimed that Jesus's human nature *captured* God. They denied that God has suffered "in the abstract" (*in abstracto*), *apart* from Christ himself. But they affirmed that God has suffered in the "concretion" of Christ (*in concreto*, in the flesh). And Pieper never understood why other Christians disagreed. "Against the Reformed," he wrote,

> we say that their almost fanatical denial of the communication of the divine attributes of God's Son to the human nature is both theological suicide and rejection of the clear Scripture teaching. . . . If the human nature of Christ, because of its finiteness, is incapable of the divine attributes of omnipotence, omniscience, and the like, then also it is incapable of the divine Person of the Son of God, who is no less infinite than is His omnipotence, omniscience, omnipresence, and the like.

Pieper was clearly peeved. He thought the gospel was at stake for, as the church had taught at least since the late fourth century, "that which he [God] has not assumed he has not healed," or, stated positively, "that which is united to the Godhead he has saved."[22] If God

21. The Monophysites arose after the Council of Chalcedon in opposition to its doctrine of the two natures of Christ. After the incarnation, they said, Christ possessed a single nature (μόνος φύσις). His humanity was swallowed up in divinity.

22. See, for example, Gregory of Nazianzus, who says, "that which He has not assumed He has not healed; but that which is united to His Godhead is also saved" in his letter "To Cledonius the Priest Against Apollinarius (*Ep.* 101)," in *Cyril of Jerusalem, Gregory Nazianzen*, vol. 7 of *Nicene and Post-Nicene Fathers*, 2nd series, ed. Philip Schaff and Henry Wace (1894; Peabody, MA: Hendrickson, 1995), 440. Athanasius expresses the same concept in his treatise *On the Incarnation of the Word*, saying, "for a sacrifice on behalf of the bodies similar to his the Word himself had also taken to himself a body," and similarly, "when man had been made and the necessity arose to heal, not the non-existent, but what had come into being, it followed that the healer and Saviour had to come among those who had already been created to cure what existed. Therefore he became a man and used the body as a human instrument. And if it was not right for it to happen in this manner, how should the Word have come when he wished to use an instrument? Or whence should he have taken it, except from those who already existed and had need of his divinity through one like them?,"

has not become human, taking sin upon himself in the person of the
Son, destroying death in his death and resurrection from the grave,
then we are miserable indeed. Reformed thinkers, Pieper fumed, did
not appreciate this fact. "In the Reformed argument against the *genus
maiestaticum*," he said, "we [face] one of the strangest aberrations
of the . . . mind. It is a yes-and-no theology, which can be explained
only by the vagaries of party spirit." The Reformed seemed uncertain
whether Jesus was really God and whether God has really triumphed
over sin, death, and the devil in the person of Jesus of Nazareth. Here
Pieper was tendentious, uncharitable, and rude. But in his fury—gospel
fury—we can see his contribution to Christology. *God* was born of
Mary, he thought. God has suffered and died for us. In Christ, God
continues to know our weakness even now.[23]

Pieper's *dolor Dei* doctrine represents a passionate God who truly
makes himself available to finite, fallen sinners, drawing near to those
who seek him in their weakness and distress. It represents a classically
Lutheran understanding of God in Christ, one epitomized famously
in the words of Dietrich Bonhoeffer, penned less than a year before his
own execution: "only the suffering God can help."[24] One would think
that this theology of the cross might preclude Christian arrogance
and carping, whether from Pieper or anyone else. However, Pieper was
so concerned to guard his precious Lutheran heritage that he rarely
engaged the suffering of those outside his church. He inculcated a
Christus dolor in an ecclesiocentric manner, railing against his Protestant peers at every step along the way. He taught a theology of the cross
triumphalistically—an irony, if not a hypocritical Christian tragedy.

---

in *Contra Gentes and De Incarnatione*, ed. and trans. Robert W. Thomson, Oxford
Early Christian Texts (Oxford: Clarendon, 1971), 157, 245.

23. Pieper treated the *genus maiestaticum* in *Christian Dogmatics*, 2:152–243.
Quotations from 154–55.

24. Bonhoeffer to Eberhard Bethge, July 16, 1944, in Dietrich Bonhoeffer, *Letters
and Papers from Prison*, rev. ed., trans. Eberhard Bethge (New York: Touchstone, 1971),
361. Cf. Dietrich Bonhoeffer, *The Cost of Discipleship*, rev. ed. (New York: Macmillan,
1959), 95–104. The most influential recent American attempt to think globally about
this Lutheran legacy is Carl E. Braaten, "The Identity and Meaning of Jesus Christ,"
in *Lutherans and the Challenge of Religious Pluralism*, ed. Frank W. Klos, C. Lynn
Nakamura, and Daniel F. Martensen (Minneapolis: Augsburg, 1990), 103–38. On the
history of such reflection in the Lutheran tradition, see Duane H. Larson, "Suffering," in *Historical Dictionary of Lutheranism*, ed. Günther Gassmann in cooperation
with Duane H. Larson and Mark W. Oldenburg, Historical Dictionaries of Religions,
Philosophies, and Movements (Lanham, MD: Scarecrow Press, 2001), 317–19.

Our contention here, then, is that this narrow and parochial treatment of Christ's redemptive work fails to account for the full significance of the incarnation of God. Although right on what matters most, it needs some help, some filling out, by other Christian views of Christ. The Lord's suffering on the cross—God's doing for us what we could not do for ourselves—is certainly of central importance for understanding the way of salvation. But we must also pay sufficient respect to other parts of the life and saving ministry of Christ, things treated much more poignantly by other theologians. Pieper's Christology proved broad and comprehensive, to be sure. But we turn to other thinkers now for helpful commentary on the many years of suffering in the life of Jesus of Nazareth *before* his final passion and crucifixion. We look at the way Reformed theology has emphasized the need for Christ to have met, throughout his lifelong incarnational mission, God's requirement of a life lived in obedience to the law. Then we listen to black Christians who have spoken most profoundly of God's presence in Jesus's many years of suffering in obedience—and in the righteous suffering of Jesus's followers.

But before we explore these sources, we want to say a word or two about terminology. In the interlude that follows, then, we clarify what we take to be an understudied difference between the way some Roman Catholics speak of God's incarnational presence through Christ in the world and the more limited, or restrained, way in which Reformed and other Protestant thinkers speak of this presence.

3

A Brief Interlude
on Incarnational Presence

Father James Martin is a well-known Catholic writer who has chronicled his spiritual pilgrimage from his early career as an executive at General Electric to his reception into the Jesuit order. At one point in his preparation for ordination, Martin spent some time working in Jamaica, working with homeless people in a hospice sponsored by Mother Teresa's Sisters of Charity. One of his duties there was to clip the toenails of those who came to the hospice for lodging, food, and health care.

Martin confesses that he regularly experienced "physical repulsion" in fulfilling his nail-clipping duties. So, in his efforts to cultivate the appropriate attitude of compassion for his Jamaican charges, he decided to think of the relationship of the suffering of Jesus to that of the individuals he was serving. But while that helped him endure some difficult assignments, he confesses that he found himself questioning "the wisdom of pretending I was helping Jesus rather than the people before me."[1]

---

1. James Martin, *In Good Company: The Fast Track from the Corporate World to Poverty, Chastity, and Obedience* (Franklin, WI: Sheed & Ward, 2010), 160.

It is highly unlikely that Mother Teresa herself would have approved of Martin's use of the notion of "pretense" in describing the presence of Jesus among the poor. When she talked about encountering Jesus on the streets of Calcutta, she typically used the language of literal presence. If people called her community of sisters an "activist" order, Mother Teresa quickly corrected them. Hers, she insisted, was a "contemplative" community, focusing on the "real presence" of Jesus both within and beyond the sacramental life of the church. Here is how she described the relationship between contemplation and serving the poor:

> I remember one of our sisters who had just come from the university. She came from a well-to-do family.
>
> As we have in our rules, the very next day after the girls have joined the society, they go to the Home for the Dying. Before they went, I told them, "You saw the priest during Mass: with what love, with what delicate care he touched the body of Christ! Make sure you do the same thing when you go to the Home, for Jesus is there in the distressing disguise."
>
> And they went.
>
> After three hours, they came back and one of them, the girl who had come from the university, who had seen so much, so many things, came to my room with such a beautiful smile on her face.
>
> She said, "For three hours I have been touching the body of Christ." And I said, "What did you do, what happened?"
>
> She said, "They brought a man from the street, covered with maggots. And I knew, though I found it very difficult, I knew that I was touching the body of Christ."[2]

Father Martin may have wished to distance himself from this appropriation of the "real presence" motif, but Mother Teresa could claim solid Catholic support for the notion that Christ's continuing incarnational presence extends well beyond sacramental celebrations. The influential Catholic ethicist Bryan Hehir, for example, justifies the public role of the Christian community theologically by appealing to the reality of the incarnation in the present day. Not only has God appeared in human history in the person of Jesus Christ, he argues, but this incarnational event is also extended "in time and space" so that God continues to "touch and transform" human reality—a process to

---

2. Mother Teresa of Calcutta, *My Life for the Poor*, ed. Jose Luis Gonzalez-Balada and Janet N. Playfoot (San Francisco: Harper & Row, 1985), 18.

which the church bears witness as it "carries the transforming grace of Christ in history."[3] Just as, for Mother Teresa, we can touch Christ by reaching our hands out to a dying leper, so also, for Hehir, we can touch him by bringing justice and peace to communities and structures.

This kind of emphasis is rather foreign to much of evangelicalism. But in strict theological terms, it is especially incompatible with the Reformed tradition, which intentionally features a restricted understanding of the incarnation. As the Heidelberg Catechism puts it, Christ is not "according to his human nature . . . now . . . upon earth," for he has taken our flesh to heaven with him as the ascended Lord, and it is from there that he presently reigns over all things "according to his Godhead, majesty, grace, and Spirit."[4]

Many Catholics would see this Calvinist insistence that Christ, in his ascension, has taken his incarnate presence with him to the heavenly regions as yet another manifestation of what they take to be an unfortunate "distancing" of God from the ordinary experiences of our lives. Father Andrew Greeley illustrates this complaint by citing the example of Bess, the heroine of Lars von Trier's film *Breaking the Waves*, who lives in a "dour" Scottish Presbyterian community. When Bess experiences a "powerful pleasure in sexual love" with her husband, Greeley reports, "she thanks God, who seems, in a grudging Calvinist way, to approve of her passion." Bess would have been better served, Greeley argues, by a "much broader Catholic view of reality" that "makes God present among us" in tangible ways.[5]

There is much to admire about the ways many Catholics, like the ones we have cited, use incarnational theology to reinforce human involvement in creation. Mother Teresa is certainly to be commended for her self-sacrificing ministry to "the poorest of the poor." And Andrew Greeley is right to encourage Bess in her desire to see her conjugal bliss as a gift from God.

The question for the Reformed tradition, then, is whether these admirable emphases that loom so large in Catholic thought and practice can be accounted for within a theological perspective, such as a

---

3. J. Bryan Hehir, "Personal Faith, the Public Church, and the Role of Theology," *Harvard Divinity Bulletin* 26, no. 1 (1996): 5.

4. Questions and answers 47 and 49 in *The Heidelberg Catechism*, in *The Creeds of Christendom, with a History and Critical Notes*, ed. Philip Schaff (Grand Rapids: Baker Books, 1996), 3:322–23.

5. Andrew Greeley, *The Catholic Imagination* (Los Angeles: University of California Press, 2000), 163, 1–2, 6.

Reformed way of viewing things, that operates with a less expansive view of the scope of the incarnation. Can such a perspective provide us with a strong sensitivity to the depths of human suffering?

When Father Martin experienced discomfort with Mother Teresa's "presence of Jesus" emphasis in serving the poor, he appropriated the idea of "pretending" to be serving Jesus when clipping the toenails of a homeless person. One way of giving this "pretense" a theological formulation from a Reformed perspective is to employ forensic terms. This is a way, for example, of construing the Savior's verdict in Matthew 25:40: "just as you did it to one of the least of these . . . you did it to me." Jesus will count the clipping of a homeless person's toenails as an act done to him. God will credit our service to the poor as an act of service to Jesus himself. It is not that Jesus is, after his ascension, still really present among the poor, but he does command his followers to serve the needy in the same manner they would perform that act of service directly to him.

To make that kind of move is to account for the admirable elements in the more comprehensive incarnationalism that Catholic thinkers set forth, without sacrificing the Reformed insistence on a more limited incarnational presence in created reality. But is this a mere exercise in "theological catch-up"—a way of demonstrating that anything that someone can say from a broad incarnationalist perspective can also be said within a Reformed theological perspective? Or is there something to commend the Reformed view as providing correctives to Catholic incarnationalism?

This question is best pursued with reference to Greeley's example of sexuality. He is certainly right to point to the repressive attitudes often associated with a "dour" Calvinism. But even at its most positive about this area of human life—a positive assessment that flows nicely from a strong doctrine of creation—Reformed thought would want to insist on taking the doctrine of radical sinfulness into account. As sinners, we human beings often stray from obedience to God's will, even in pursuing very ordinary pleasures. We are rebels, fallen creatures, and this means that every aspect of creation is touched by sin. And because we are so convinced of the all-pervasive character of human sinfulness, Calvinists have made it a special spiritual-theological calling to keep reminding other Christians that there is no dimension of our created life that does not afford a real—and often deceptively subtle—opportunity for disobedience to the will of God. Is the erotic aspect of our lives a part of the creation that God originally called good? Yes, of course. But there is also the real danger that under sinful conditions the erotic can become a staging area for a violation of the Creator's purposes. Our sexuality is one of the many aspects of fallen nature that needs to be redeemed.

So, Reformed thought resists issuing any carte blanche endorsement of our "natural" yearnings and pleasures. For Christians, the term "natural" should always require some unpacking before we can engage in any discussion of human realities. "Natural" can refer to our created nature. In this sense it is perfectly legitimate to say that we human beings are "by nature good." But we can also use "natural" to refer to our fallen condition, and in that sense it is also important to say that we are "by nature sinful."

But again, the positive dimensions are also emphasized within Reformed thought. Susan Schreiner captures this emphasis nicely in the title she chose for her study of John Calvin's view of how the natural order points us to the Creator: *The Theater of His Glory*. To be sure, as Schreiner points out, Calvin did insist that nature's order was a fragile affair and that the tendency toward disorder is so great that only the active ordering of God could provide stability. But Calvin also celebrated the faithfulness of a God who continually delights in the created works that he holds together by his sovereign power, so that our joy is, in fact, a participation in the divine joy.[6]

God's relationship to his creation, however, is certainly not a matter of unmitigated joy. God also identifies with the very real—and extensive—patterns of human suffering. The fact of that identification is an important component of Reformed theology. But it has not always been explicitly attended to—at least not in the way that Mother Teresa and others have described it in their experience. One way to guarantee the right sort of attention is to look at an example of how God's identification with human suffering has been downplayed. So we turn now to Charles Hodge, a prominent Reformed theologian in America who treated the redemptive suffering of Christ at length without any sustained focus on the broad sufferings of humanity. From there we will also explore other models—both insufficient and constructive—within the Reformed tradition for formulating a compassionate Christology that upholds the tradition's core theological commitments.

---

6. Susan E. Schreiner, *The Theater of His Glory: Nature and the Natural Order in the Thought of John Calvin*, 2nd ed. (Grand Rapids: Baker Books, 1995).

4

Reformed Theology
and the Suffering of Christ

We have already pointed out that the Reformed tradition has
been critical of the ways that other theological systems treat the
incarnation. These criticisms extend not only to Roman Catholicism,
where the incarnation is often portrayed as a general and ongoing
joining of the divine with created reality, but also to Lutheranism,
with the kind of *Christus dolor* emphases we have seen at work in
earlier chapters. We will look below at the actual ways in which Reformed theologians have typically depicted the incarnation, attempt-
ing to probe at what exactly gives rise to the passion that has often
characterized Reformed polemics on this subject. We will also look
for theological resources within the Reformed tradition—however
underutilized they have often been—that can provide a more expansive
account of the sufferings of Christ.

Charles Hodge

The incarnational suffering of Christ is a central theme in Charles
Hodge's theological system. But Hodge does much stage-setting before
he gets around to that subject. In his classic *Systematic Theology*,

Hodge sets out, after a detailed treatment of methodology, to discuss
the being and nature of God, focusing initially on the way in which
God, who is a Spirit, "is distinguished from all other spirits in that
he is infinite, eternal, unchangeable in his being and perfections."
These attributes of God as eternal Spirit require us also to see him,
Hodge argues, as "a person—a self-conscious, intelligent, voluntary
agent." He then points to the classic notion of divine simplicity, which
stipulates that "nothing can either be added to, or taken from God."[1]

Pursuing at length that kind of discussion regarding the doctrine
of God proper, it takes Hodge another hundred pages to get around
to talking about the incarnational ministry of the Second Person of
the Trinity. And even then he is primarily concerned to demonstrate
Christ's full divinity—which means, Hodge insists, that even in his
human form, Jesus had full "control over nature." The miracles he
performed, says Hodge, were performed with a divine power that
he continued to possess in his incarnate state. Having introduced
the subject of Christ's humanity, it takes Hodge over another five
hundred pages before he attends to the fact that Jesus had a very real
physical body. Almost one hundred pages after that, Hodge finally
arrives at the subject of the suffering of Christ. But even when he deals
with Christ's incarnational self-emptying and suffering, he focuses
almost exclusively on Christ's suffering at the very end of his life, the
vicarious suffering of the cross.[2] In the light of the views laid out in
the previous chapters, it is important to observe this focus. Hodge
gives almost no attention to the suffering of Jesus during the earlier
stages of his life.

But we must note the "*almost* no" factor here. At one point Hodge
does briefly refer to the sufferings of Jesus prior to the cross, and,
significantly, he does so in his polemics against the Lutheran understanding of the joining of the divine and human natures in the
incarnation. What Hodge finds particularly disturbing in Lutheran
writings on the subject is captured in a comment that he cites from the
German Lutheran theologian Isaac August Dorner. Dorner appeals to
the viewpoint of some Tübingen dogmaticians to argue that "the act
of incarnation communicates the divine essence to humanity" in such
a way that, for example, the attribute of omnipresence is "actually,"

1. Charles Hodge, *Systematic Theology* (1871–1872; New York: Scribner,
1872–1873), 1:367, 379.
    2. Ibid., 1:503–4; 2:381, 475–76.

and not just potentially—"not merely its potence"—directly "communicated to the flesh of Christ."[3]

Hodge's verdict on this portrayal is harsh. Such a view, he says, "supposes the whole earthly life of Christ to be an illusion." It takes for granted that the infant Jesus in the manger was already all-knowing and all-powerful. Indeed, on this kind of perspective, says Hodge, "He was the ruler of the universe cooperating in all of the activity of the Logos when in the womb of the Virgin." This would mean that "he never suffered or died, and there has been no redemption through his blood."[4]

Hodge does immediately go on to recognize that Lutheran theologians typically looked for a way of avoiding the implications he was charging them with. Some of them insisted that the divine nature was only there potentially throughout the earthly ministry. Others talked about a "veiling" of Christ's divinity. But, argues Hodge, none of these concepts really helped the situation. The only plausible option, Hodge insists, is to keep to the particularities of the incarnation: that in Jesus the Son of Man joined himself to a specific "true body and a reasonable soul." As a result of that joining, he "was, and continues to be, God and man, in two entire and distinct natures, and one person forever. Whatever is beyond this, is mere speculation."[5]

At the heart of what Hodge sees as Lutheran "speculation" regarding the incarnation is Christ's presence in humanity *in general*. He rejects the insistence that "in virtue of the incarnation the attributes of the divine nature were communicated to the human, so that wherever the Logos is there the soul and body of Christ must be."[6] This means that, since the Bethlehem baby was the incarnation of the divine Logos, that child was already omnipotent and omniscient. And even more troubling, having joined divinity to humanity as such, Christ continues to be present in all of humanity in his present status as the risen and exalted Lord.

It is in rejecting the wedding of the divine with humanity in this manner that Hodge offers a strong but brief affirmation of the ways in which Christ, throughout his earthly life, suffered—not just on behalf of, but *in solidarity with*, humankind:

3. Ibid., 2:412. Hodge is citing I. A. Dorner, *History of the Development of the Doctrine of the Person of Christ*, div. 2, vol. 2 (Edinburgh: T&T Clark, 1862), 284.
4. Hodge, *Systematic Theology*, 2:412.
5. Ibid., 414.
6. Ibid.

If anything is plainly revealed in the Scriptures concerning our Lord, and if there is anything to which the heart of the believer instinctively clings, it is that although He is God over all and blessed forever, He is nevertheless a man like ourselves; bone of our bone, and flesh of our flesh; one who can be touched with a sense of our infirmities; and who knows from his own experience and present consciousness, what a weak and infirm thing human nature is. . . . [He is] our Saviour, the Jesus of the Bible, who was a man of sorrows and acquainted with grief, who was one with us in his humanity, and therefore can sympathize with us and save us.[7]

Here we have a bold and straightforward affirmation of the overall point we are stressing in this discussion. Hodge rightly highlights the fact that the suffering on the cross, by means of which the Son of God accomplished for us what we could not accomplish for ourselves, was necessarily preceded by decades of suffering that he experienced in solidarity with us: he had to suffer in ways that we suffer in order then to take on the unique suffering that he alone could bear as our sinless Savior.

This theme comes through so clearly at this point in Hodge's theological explorations because of two emphases that are prominent in Reformed theology. One emphasis, as clearly displayed in Hodge's discussion here, is the Calvinist nervousness about any metaphysical "speculation" that takes us beyond what is clearly stated in Scripture. The notion of the divine permanently joining itself to human nature in general is a case in point for that kind of speculation. What is clear from the biblical account, Hodge insists, is that the Second Person of the Trinity took humanity upon himself specifically in the person of Jesus of Nazareth.

The second emphasis has to do with the Reformed highlighting of the divine requirement that the transaction at Calvary had to be accomplished by one who fulfilled the demands of God's law. The sinless One was the fully obedient One—revealing to us what it is like for a human life to be lived in conformity to the demands of holiness as set forth in the Mosaic law. While this emphasis is not necessarily absent in other traditions, it comes to the fore in the particular way that Reformed thought understands the close, and positive, relationship between law and gospel.

Our main problem with Hodge's treatment of this subject of Christ's empathic suffering—the suffering that Christ shares with

7. Ibid., 417.

all humanity—is its placement in his overall treatment of Christology. His bold affirmation of Christ's sharing in our suffering occurs in the context of a polemical critique of Lutheran thought on the two natures. And even there it shows up primarily as an illustration of the dangers of engaging in metaphysical speculation regarding the relationship of the divine to the human. But in his lengthy systematic discussion of the major aspects of Christ's atoning work, where Hodge addresses at length the suffering of the Son of God, he focuses only on the final stage of the earthly redemptive mission, emphasizing the ways in which Christ's suffering was very much unlike our own.

Hodge is not alone in the Reformed tradition in his failure to give much attention to the significance of Christ's sufferings prior to the final days of his redemptive mission. John Calvin himself exhibits the same pattern in his *Institutes of the Christian Religion*. Christ had to be fully human, Calvin insists in his discussion of the incarnation, so that he could "present our flesh as the price of satisfaction to God's righteous judgment, and, in the same flesh, to pay the penalty that we had deserved."[8]

It is significant for our discussion that Calvin moves immediately from this concise statement of the meaning of Christ's suffering to a lengthy discussion of why the incarnation was necessary—and in doing so, he engages in a polemic against the views of Andreas Osiander, a Lutheran theologian.[9] The sole reason why God took on our human nature in Christ, Calvin argues, is "to restore the fallen world and to succor lost men." This means, he goes on, that we must guard carefully against those theologians—here Calvin has Osiander particularly in his sights—who contend that the incarnation would have occurred even if the fall had not happened. This is just another example, Calvin argues, of those "vague speculations that captivate the frivolous and the seekers after novelty." And in this case, Calvin insists, the speculation contradicts the clear teaching of Scripture as set forth in Christ's specification of his incarnational mission in Matthew 18:11: "the Son of Man came to save what has been lost."[10]

8. John Calvin, *Institutes of the Christian Religion*, trans. Ford Lewis Battles, ed. John T. McNeill (Philadelphia: Westminster, 1960), 2.12.3.

9. For an English-language introduction to Osiander and his thought, see Gottfried Seebass, "Osiander, Andreas," in *The Oxford Encyclopedia of the Reformation*, ed. Hans J. Hillerbrand (New York: Oxford University Press, 1996), 3:183–85.

10. Calvin, *Institutes*, 2.12.4.

Throughout his discussion of matters pertaining to the incarnation, Calvin regularly refers to the sufferings that the Savior experienced in years prior to the final days leading to the crucifixion. But even when he mentions those themes, Calvin's thoughts are never far from Jesus's triumph. For example, when he explains that by joining "human nature with divine" Jesus was taking our "weakness" upon himself, Calvin quickly adds the reason why the Son did so—namely, that in his divinity "he might win victory for us."[11] Like Hodge, Calvin's thoughts about the incarnation are never far removed from the motif of triumph. Jesus had to undergo the deepest agonies of the human condition in order to demonstrate that even under the most difficult of circumstances he did not fall into sin—only in doing so could he win the victory over sin and death.

The "Lingering" Corrective

To further clarify our concern here, it is not that Hodge and Calvin leave no room at all for Christ's "identifying-with" human suffering. Nor is the problem that when they do point to empathic suffering they see it as a necessary step toward the suffering of the cross. When Calvin discusses what Christ had to do in preparation for the work of Calvary, for example, he mentions the assurance of the writer to the Hebrews, that "we do not have a high priest who is unable to sympathize with our weaknesses" (Heb. 4:15). In doing so he acknowledges a vital biblical truth: Christ had to be like us in order to offer himself up as a sacrifice for our sins.

The identifying-with aspect of Christ's suffering was an important means toward the goal of going to the cross. But it was not a mere means, as if we can skip quickly over it in our theology, moving to a discussion of the "real" point of the incarnation, the final redemptive transaction at Calvary. The identifying-with concept has its own value, theologically and spiritually. It needs its own attention as an important teaching. It is an aspect of the incarnation that is important to linger over. One important feature of the incarnational ministry of Jesus is that a member of the divine Trinity came to earth to understand—from the "inside" of our humanness—what it is like to be one of us in our frailty.

The habit of moving too quickly over that empathic aspect of Christ's suffering shows up elsewhere in Reformed thought. For

11. Ibid., 2.12.3.

example, the Dutch-American Calvinist theologian Louis Berkhof, in his *Systematic Theology*—a much-used theological text in conservative Reformed circles in twentieth-century North America—devotes several pages to Christ's suffering. Berkhof acknowledges at the start that "in view of the fact that Jesus began to speak of his coming sufferings towards the end of his life, we are often inclined to think that the final agonies constituted the whole of his sufferings." This is unfortunate, says Berkhof, because it fails to acknowledge that "his whole life was a life of suffering."[12]

Having offered his corrective, Berkhof goes on to argue that, while the basic reason for the necessity of the Savior's lifelong suffering is "that he took the place of sinners vicariously," there are also four "proximate causes" of that suffering that should be taken into account:

1. He who was Lord of the universe had to occupy a menial position, even the position of bond-servant or slave, and he who had an inherent right to command was in duty bound to obey.

2. He who was pure and holy had to live in a sinful, polluted atmosphere, in daily association with sinners, and was constantly reminded of the greatness of the guilt with which he was burdened by the sins of his contemporaries.

3. He had perfect awareness and clear anticipation, from the very beginning of his life, of the extreme sufferings that would, as it were, overwhelm him in the end. He knew exactly what was coming, and the outlook was far from cheerful.

4. Finally, also, he suffered privations of life, temptations of the devil, hatred and rejection of the people, and maltreatment and persecutions.[13]

Not one word here points to a desire in the Savior to empathize with—to act in solidarity with—the sufferings of human beings in general. Indeed, having offered this set of "proximate causes," Berkhof immediately goes on to warn that, while we sometimes talk of Christ's participation in humanity's "ordinary" sufferings, the Savior's agonies throughout his life "had an extraordinary character

12. Louis Berkhof, *Systematic Theology*, 4th rev. and enlarged ed. (Grand Rapids: Eerdmans, 1959), 336–37.
13. Ibid., 337.

in his case, and were therefore unique."[14] This statement can easily detract from the fact that Berkhof appreciated the necessity of Jesus's lifelong sufferings.

This same kind of emphasis on the uniqueness of Christ's "ordinary" sufferings shows up in many of the continental Dutch Reformed theologians. Abraham Kuyper, for one, in a meditation on the pre-Calvary agonies of Christ, also highlights the ways in which those sufferings must be seen as anticipating the unique anguish of the cross. All the travail that Christ experienced earlier in his life, Kuyper observes, "forecasts the underlying melody of the heavenly-composed theme of redemption. Each step toward Calvary brought him nearer to the sound of singing believers rejoicing in the blood that had been shed for their salvation."[15] Similarly, Klaas Schilder wrote a lengthy book on the subject of Christ's sufferings, with chapter titles like these: "Christ's Sorrows Have Their Own Peculiar Origin," "Christ's Sorrows Have Their Own Peculiar Cause," "Christ's Sorrows Have Their Own Peculiar End," and so on—the point being that Christ's sorrows are consistently unlike what other human beings experience.[16]

Why is there this failure in so much of Reformed theology to linger over the shared-sufferings aspect of Christ's incarnational mission? We have already seen one important factor: the Reformed tradition sees as its special obligation to keep the teachings about the incarnation within definite theological bounds. Against those theologies that want to extend the incarnation temporally and spatially, the Reformed have regularly argued that the earthly incarnation came to an end with Christ's ascension to heaven. As Richard Muller has observed, "Reformed Christology has always insisted not only on the resurrection of Christ's body but also on the heavenly location and finitude of Christ's resurrected humanity. Christ now sits at the right hand of God and visibly rules the church triumphant." The danger of the more metaphysically inclined view, Muller argues, is that "it detracts from the majesty of the doctrine of Christ's kingship."[17]

Muller's reference to a concern for "majesty" in this context is one more clue for understanding the Reformed reluctance to linger

14. Ibid., 337.
15. Abraham Kuyper, *His Decease at Jerusalem* (Grand Rapids: Eerdmans, 1946), 14.
16. Klaas Schilder, *Christ in His Suffering*, trans. Henry Zylstra (Grand Rapids: Eerdmans, 1938).
17. Richard Muller, "How Many Points?" *Calvin Theological Journal* 28, no. 2 (November 1993): 430.

over Christ's empathic suffering. Reformed theology has, more than any other tradition, said much about divine *sovereignty*. Calvinism has typically highlighted the great ontological gap between Creator and creature. The Calvinist insistence on God's absolute sovereign purposes in providence and election are obvious cases in point. But the sovereignty emphasis also has direct relevance, in Reformed minds, to a proper understanding of the incarnation. We will look now at that connection, as it bears on the broader question of the ontological gap between God and his creation.

Distance and Nearness

Jelle Faber explores the ways that various Dutch Calvinist thinkers have opposed the idea that the incarnation would have occurred even if the need for redemption had not emerged, and in doing so Faber points to the Creator-creature union/distinction as a controlling concern. As an especially telling case in point, he cites Klaas Schilder's rejection of any theology of the incarnation that suggests some sort of ontological "attraction" between the divine and human natures, as if the two were somehow "infatuated with each other."[18]

While the insistence on an unbridgeable ontological gap is fundamental to all expressions of traditional Christian teaching, the Reformed have seen it as their special calling to protect that gap against any doctrine that might seem to compromise it. Thus the typical Calvinist emphasis on God the *totaliter aliter* who reigns supreme over all things and who, in the words of the Westminster Confession, "worketh when, and where, and how he pleaseth," including the ways in which he sovereignly dispenses electing grace.[19] And it is not difficult to understand how the idea of the inevitability of the incarnation could be seen as compromising the notion of an unbridgeable ontological gap. The incarnational theology of the twentieth-century Jesuit theologian Karl Rahner offers a clear case in point. We cannot understand "the God-Man," Rahner argues, "simply as someone who

18. Jelle Faber, *Essays in Reformed Doctrine* (Neerlandia, AB: Inheritance Publications, 1990), 51. In citing Schilder, Faber is translating comments from Schilder's *Heidelbergsche Catechismus* (Goes: Osterbaan & Le Cointre, 1949), 2:93.

19. "The Westminster Confession of Faith," 10.3, "Of Effectual Calling," in *The Creeds of Christendom, with a History and Critical Notes*, ed. Philip Schaff (Grand Rapids: Baker Books, 1996), 3:625.

enters into our existence and its history from the outside, moves it a step further and also brings it to fulfillment in a certain sense, but then nevertheless leaves it behind." Rather, in the incarnation, something happens to God in God's own *being*—in Christ, "God brings about man's self-transcendence into God," resulting in a unity that is not only a "'moral' unity," but "an irrevocable kind of unity between this human reality and God."[20]

Given this kind of formulation, it is easy to see why Charles Hodge, in looking at the historical development of incarnation theology, warned that a theory like Osiander's has "at last found its adequate scientific expression by Schleiermacher and Hegel, that Christ as Redeemer is the perfected creation of human nature; or that the divine nature is the truth of humanity, and human nature the reality, or existence form (*die Wirklichkeit*) of the divine nature."[21]

It is worth mentioning again—as was noted in an earlier chapter—that Nevin, as a Reformed thinker, seemed occasionally to show some sympathy for the idea of the necessity of the incarnation. And he even gave a favorable review to the writings on the subject by Julius Müller—this at a time when he was especially sensitive to criticisms that he was leaning too far in a "Catholic" direction in his thought in general. But still, he never actually endorsed this doctrine, perhaps because of the Reformed influence on his thought, leaving it ultimately to the realm of "mystery."[22]

Reformed theologians also sought to keep the incarnation within certain theological bounds because they resisted the suggestion in other theological systems, which we have already seen, that Christ somehow "joined" himself to humanity in general in taking on human form, even though they understood the incarnation solely in remedial or salvific terms. This issue loomed large in Charles Hodge's critique of Nevin's book *Mystical Presence*, where Hodge took Nevin to task for suggesting that Christ's incarnation brought about an infusion

20. Karl Rahner, *Foundations of Christian Faith: An Introduction to the Idea of Christianity* (New York: Crossroad, 2002), 200–202.

21. Hodge, *Systematic Theology*, 3:182. Hodge is quoting from F. C. Baur's *Die christliche Lehre von der Versöhnung in ihrer geschichtlichen Entwicklung bis auf die neueste Zeit* [The Christian doctrine of the atonement in its historical development up to the present time] (Tübingen: Verlag von C. F. Osiander, 1838), 330n.

22. For an account of Nevin's wavering on this matter, see D. G. Hart, *John Williamson Nevin: High-Church Calvinist*, American Reformed Biographies (Phillipsburg, NJ: P&R, 2005), 146–49.

of new life into humankind in general. For Hodge, this suggestion violates the Calvinist understanding of election. If the benefits of the incarnation are primarily salvific, and if not all human beings are saved, what are we to make of a kind of spiritual gift going out to the whole human race by virtue of God's incarnate presence within the created order?[23]

This question in turn highlights the centrality of the forensic in the Reformed understanding of the incarnation. The coming of the Savior was intended for the salvation of the lost—and that salvation extends only to the elect. Any suggestion, then, that the incarnation imparted something beneficial to all human beings is troubling for Reformed thinkers. The ultimate goal of Christ's earthly ministry was to declare a subset of humanity righteous, solely because of the redemptive transaction that took place on Calvary. Everything else—the infancy of Jesus, his youthful years, his mighty acts and teachings during his public ministry, along with the resurrection and ascension—has to be understood with reference to his accomplishing what sinful human beings could not accomplish in their own strength. He became weak so that redeemed sinners might share in the victory that he alone could accomplish.

Corrective Steps

What kinds of corrective moves might be made within Reformed thought, without violating the basic concerns underlying the Calvinist critique of other traditions? An important place to focus is on the idea of sovereignty and how it has been construed within various strands of Reformed thought, bearing on the distance-nearness relationship between God and humankind.

In her 1994 book *Orthodoxies in Massachusetts*, Janice Knight distinguishes between two schools of thought within the orthodox Calvinism of American Puritanism. The subtitle of Knight's book, "Rereading American Puritanism," signals the revisionist intent of her discussion—as does the main title itself, which is a deliberate play on the title of Perry Miller's classic 1933 work, *Orthodoxy in Massachusetts 1630–1650*. In Miller's depiction, Puritanism portrayed

---

23. Hodge's concerns on this issue are summarized by Hart in *John Williamson Nevin*, 127–28, from Hodge's review essay, "Doctrine of the Reformed Church on the Lord's Supper," *Biblical Repertory and Princeton Review* 20 (1848): 227–78.

God as a distant sovereign before whom human beings must live in reverence in the presence of transcendent mystery. William Ames was a dominant influence in setting forth this conception, advocating a pattern of spirituality in which the believer's relationship to God was dominated by metaphors like master/servant and king/subject. To be sure, a "warmer" piety often showed up in this context, but always against the background that everything else had to be understood with reference to God as "an exacting lord" and a "demanding covenanter."[24]

Knight finds a significant alternative within Puritanism to Ames's conception of sovereign power as the primary attribute of God. She details the ways in which some American Puritans looked to Richard Sibbes, Ames's contemporary in Old England, for their theological inspiration. The Sibbesians offered a Calvinist conception of God in whom mercy and not power was primary. Here was a clear alternative to the Amesian view of a deity to whom, as Knight puts it, "the only bridge was the contractual covenant, not the personal Christ."[25]

Sibbesian Calvinism played down the notion of divine sovereignty in favor of images of intimacy, as in Sibbes's assurance that God

> applies himself to us, and hath taken upon himself near relations, that he might be near us in goodness. He is a father, and everywhere to maintain us. He is a husband, and everywhere to help. He is a friend, and everywhere to comfort and counsel. So his love it is a near love. Therefore he has taken upon him the nearest relations, that we may never want God and the testimonies of his love.[26]

What is especially significant about Knight's exposition of these competing Calvinist conceptions of God is that each conception generates a different understanding of the incarnation. While Knight does not elaborate on this matter, she does provide us with a helpful clue that deserves elaboration. She cites the claim of John Eusden, who edited a recent edition of Ames's *Marrow of Theology*, that "the Christocentrism of Martin Luther is not shared by most English

24. Janice Knight, *Orthodoxies in Massachusetts: Rereading American Puritanism* (Cambridge: Harvard University Press, 1994), 78.

25. Ibid., 77.

26. Richard Sibbes, *The Complete Works of Richard Sibbes* (Edinburgh: J. Nichol, 1862–1864), 4:196; quoted by Knight, *Orthodoxies*, 83.

Puritans," which means, says Eusden, that for Puritanism Christ's incarnation "was not a mystery in which man should lose himself."[27]

But, of course, this avoidance of a Lutheran type of christocentrism holds true primarily, as Knight tells the story, for Amesian Puritanism. The somewhat different conception of the divine attributes as set forth by the Sibbesians suggests the possibility of a view of the incarnation that allows for a more comprehensive understanding of the compassionate Christ.

There is no need here, in following a more Sibbesian version of Calvinism, to abandon the central emphasis on divine sovereignty. The Sibbesians certainly never abandoned it. Rather, they looked for an alternative to an *arbitrary* sovereignty. The divine Friend still chooses his beloved ones out of sovereign grace, and his love to believers is not something that can be demanded of him. Nor was the incarnation of the Son, on such a view, anything but a gift of that sovereign love.

The Grounds of Divine Compassion

We should state explicitly that both of these conceptions, the Amesian and the Sibbesian, are compatible with the rudiments of the Reformed confessional tradition. They each comport well with the way that, for example, the Westminster Confession positions the incarnational ministry of Christ against the background of God's absolute sovereignty.

In outlining the key role of God's covenantal dealings with humankind, Westminster begins by insisting upon the link between sovereignty and incarnation.[28] "The distance between God and the creature is so great," says Westminster, that fellowship with the Creator can only occur "by some voluntary condescension on God's part, which he hath been pleased to express by way of covenant." This expression originally—in the garden—took the form of a "covenant of works," requiring humans' "perfect and personal obedience" to the commands of God.

When the conditions for implementation of the covenant of works failed because of human rebellion, the Confession goes on, "the

27. Knight, *Orthodoxies*, 77. Knight is quoting John D. Eusden's introduction to *Marrow of Theology: William Ames, 1576–1633* (Boston: Pilgrim Press, 1968).

28. The account here of the Confession's treatment of the covenant follows the line of argument in "Westminster Confession," 7.1–3 and 8.2, 4, and 5, in Schaff, *Creeds of Christendom*, 3:616–17, 619–21.

Lord was pleased to make a second, commonly called the covenant of grace; wherein he freely offered unto sinners life and salvation by Jesus Christ." This arrangement, in turn, required that the divine Son "did, when the fullness of time was come, take upon him man's nature, with all the essential properties and common infirmities thereof, yet without sin." Christ took this incarnational ministry upon himself "under the law, and he did perfectly fulfill it," and in doing so, he "endured most grievous torments immediately in his soul, and most painful sufferings in his body."

In this reference to Christ's "most grievous torments" and "most painful sufferings" it seems clear that the Westminster divines are thinking primarily of the final week of his passion—the sufferings of Gethsemane and Golgotha. But the previous years of Christ's earthly life are at least acknowledged formally when the Confession goes on to observe that it was by both "his perfect obedience and sacrifice of himself" that he was able to satisfy the demands of divine justice.

Again, both the Amesian and the Sibbesian perspectives can be seen as equally legitimate ways of spelling out the meaning of Christ's incarnational ministry. What we are looking for, however, is the Reformed viewpoint that best gives us explicit incarnational grounds for a compassionate Christology. And here the Sibbesian viewpoint is the likely option.   ·

What we see in the Westminster presentation of incarnational suffering is an acknowledgment that the final suffering of Christ was redemptively effective only because he had lived a life of perfect conformity to God's creating designs for human flourishing. But what often gets emphasized—as is the case with the Westminster portrayal—is the way Christ's suffering differs from ours: he endured horrible agonies, unlike us, in the context of a sinless humanness. What we fail to see spelled out at any length in much traditional Reformed thought, though, is the affirmation that his suffering was also *like* ours—an identification *with* the deepest hurts and hopes of the human condition.

That this requirement of incarnational solidarity with shared human suffering is not foreign to Reformed thought can be seen in the many examples of genuine Christlike concern for the poor. We need look no further than John Calvin in this regard. Calvin was very concerned to restore the office of deacon to what he argued was the biblical linkage between the diaconate and service to the poor—a connection that he argued had been lost in Catholic practice. In making his case in the *Institutes*, he endorses some rather strong claims of Ambrose, such as, "The church has gold not to keep but to pay out, and to relieve distress"; "Whatever, then, the church had was for the support of the needy"; and "The bishop had nothing that did not belong to the poor."[29]

What is absent in these genuine expressions of concern for the needy, though, is that those concerns be grounded in Christ's incarnational identification with human neediness. Calvin wants the church to conform to biblical teachings about serving the poor. Kuyper, as we shall see below, moves in a more explicitly christological direction by pointing out that Christ, like the ancient prophets, called for justice for the poor. But neither says anything about Christ actually *experiencing* the marginalization and pain of those who suffer.

Christ's Empathic Suffering

In our effort to articulate an incarnationally grounded Reformed understanding of Christ's suffering-with human beings, we can leave much of what we have seen as characteristic of Reformed theology intact—with the proviso that we are drawing upon the Sibbesian rather than the Amesian conception regarding divine sovereignty. We can preserve the "redemption-only" feature as the central purpose of the incarnation, as well as the strong employment of forensic categories in explaining the work of Calvary. And we can view the incarnation as "contained" within an earthly ministry of Christ that culminated in his taking our human nature with him to heaven.

All of this is to say that we need to make no apology for keeping the basic intentions of the Calvinist approach to the incarnation intact. But we do need to supplement the teachings based on those intentions with resources that give us a more robust and extensive view of the compassion of Christ.

And here there is at least one classically Calvinistic writer who actually comes very close to providing the necessary supplement. In a powerful address delivered to a Christian Social Congress in 1891, Abraham Kuyper spoke fervently about God's concern for the poor, and more particularly about Jesus's advocacy for the concerns of the poor. To be sure, Kuyper also insisted that we should not romanticize the poor—all of us are sinners, he noted. But nonetheless, Kuyper

29. Calvin, *Institutes*, 4.4.8.

observed, when the Bible "corrects the poor [it] does so much more tenderly and gently; and in contrast, when it call[s] the rich to account [it] uses much harsher words."[30]

This statement does not go beyond Calvin's pleas on behalf of the poor. Kuyper too has grounded the concern for the needy in the obligation to obey what God has commanded in his Word. And what he points to in Jesus's example is his advocacy for the poor.

But at one point in his speech Kuyper expands his focus on the example of Jesus by pointing his hearers to the Savior's compassion. And he makes his case with eloquence:

> Jesus works not only through moral motivation. He preaches through his *personal life*. When rich and poor stand opposed to each other, he never takes his place with the wealthier, but always stands with the poorer. He is born in a stable; and while foxes have holes and birds have nests, the Son of Man has nowhere to lay his head. . . . Powerful is the trait of pity, which is imprinted on every page of the Gospel where Jesus comes in contact with the suffering and oppressed. He does not thrust aside the unlearned masses, but draws them to him. He would extinguish no wick that even barely smoulders. Whatever is sick is cured by him. He does not hold back his hand from the touch of leprous flesh. When the multitude hunger, even though as yet they do not hunger for the bread of life, he breaks the loaf into many pieces and gives them an abundance of precious fish.[31]

That comes very close to our purposes. But two matters need special unpacking from what Kuyper says about the Savior's compassion.

One matter that needs to be made explicit is that the attainment of the compassion that Kuyper is describing is indeed one of the key purposes of the incarnation. God in Christ wanted to become one of us in order to *experience* what it means to *be* a human immersed in the brokenness of a fallen world. To say that is to capture an important biblical truth, and saying it does not compromise any basic conviction associated with Reformed theology.

The other matter relates directly to an important weakness that we have already identified in many treatments of Christ's suffering—namely, a restricted focus on what that suffering means for the Christian

---

30. Abraham Kuyper, *Christianity and the Class Struggle*, trans. Dirk Jellema (Grand Rapids: Piet Heyn Publishers, 1950), 29n13.
31. Ibid., 27–28.

community in a way that ignores, or even explicitly denies, any application to humanity in general. Kuyper clearly wants to correct this restricted focus, addressing the plight of people who are beyond the boundaries of the believing community. Jesus, he says, has compassion on people who "as yet . . . do not hunger for the bread of life"—and he feeds them. And one does not need to engage in much speculation to suggest that many of those whom Jesus fed physically *never* actually reached out to him to satisfy themselves with the spiritual food that he came to provide.

Jesus was not dispensing his miraculous benefits throughout his earthly ministry with the distinction between "elect" and "non-elect" in mind. Nor does he call us to show compassion to others only with reference to those categories. Indeed, the compassion of Jesus is a broad compassion that he also mandates for his disciples:

> If you love those who love you, what credit is that to you? For even sinners love those who love them. If you do good to those who do good to you, what credit is that to you? For even sinners do the same. If you lend to those from whom you hope to receive, what credit is that to you? Even sinners lend to sinners, to receive as much again. But love your enemies, do good, and lend, expecting nothing in return. Your reward will be great, and you will be children of the Most High; for he is kind to the ungrateful and the wicked.
>
> Luke 6:32–35

In mandating this kindness toward even "the ungrateful and the wicked," Jesus is teaching something that, as Kuyper puts it, the Savior "preaches through His *personal life*." Indeed, the most amazing example of his compassion even for his enemies is seen on the cross when, in the midst of the time of his greatest agony, he cries out, "Father, forgive them; for they do not know what they are doing" (Luke 23:34).

Taking the Next Step

We have been able, in discussing the views of Lutheran and Reformed theologians, to find theological resources for a compassionate Christology. But we must confess that finding those resources does take some work. In some cases we find good theology that nonetheless makes no explicit mention of a Savior whose redemptive ministry required that he identify with the agonies of the human condition, not only to have victory over them, but also simply to understand the cries of those who desperately long for what is contained in the victory. Other theologians do touch on the importance of Christlike compassion, but fail to see the need to extend it beyond the boundaries of their own world of familiar relationships. And then there are those who do finally give us grounds for seeking out a broader Christlike compassion, but only after we expend energy in teasing out those grounds from their formulations regarding the incarnation.

It is not insignificant that in the case of Abraham Kuyper, he was most articulate on our subject when he stood before an audience of common laborers. He could speak most eloquently about a Savior who broke very real bread for the hungry masses when he actually faced a gathering of listeners for whom access to the means of providing for their families with daily bread was often an urgent struggle.

What this should tell us is that our formal theological prescriptions need to be more interactive with an immersion in the realities of the human condition. Fortunately, we have profound models of this kind of theological reflection—models that we can see only if we look beyond the walls of theological studies to environs where believers have engaged in theological struggle as they have walked lonely paths of rejection and pain. We turn now to one of those contexts from which we have learned much in our own journeys: the life of faith nurtured within the African American slave communities.

5

Christus Dolor among the Slaves and Their Descendants

The South is crucifying Christ again
By all the laws of ancient rote and rule:
The ribald cries of "Save yourself" and "Fool"
Din in his ears, the thorns grope for his brain,
And where they bite, swift springing rivers stain
His gaudy, purple robe of ridicule
With sullen red; and acid wine to cool
His thirst is thrust at him, with lurking pain.
Christ's awful wrong is that he's dark of hue,
The sin for which no blamelessness atones;
But lest the sameness of the cross should tire,
They kill him now with famished tongues of fire,
And while he burns, good men, and women, too,
Shout, battling for his black and brittle bones.

Countee P. Cullen[1]

The Reformation traditions that have shaped American Christology have historically accented the triumphant notes of divine

1. Countee P. Cullen, "Christ Recrucified," *Kelley's Magazine* (October 1922): 13, as reprinted in Jean Wagner, ed., *Black Poets of the United States: From Paul Laurence Dunbar to Langston Hughes* (Urbana: University of Illinois Press, 1973), 335. For more

sovereignty, majesty, and power. Regarding the cross, then, the emphasis traditionally falls on Christ's supernatural victory over sin, death, and the devil. In the previous chapters we have attempted to demonstrate that beneath these themes of triumph in both the Reformed and Lutheran traditions run deep undertones of suffering, grief, and the association of Christ with the human condition. The theologians we have highlighted all understood, to varying degrees, the significance of the incarnation and the suffering of God in Christ for theology. Some played a role in pulling these themes out of the background and into a position of prominence in their theological work, as well as in their own Christian lives and ministries. Even so, the themes of Christ's suffering, and of God's suffering in Christ, remain subordinate in American christological formulas. This may be due to the fact that even for strident defenders of a *Christus dolor* theology, such as Franz Pieper, the suffering of Christ and God in Christ—the "man of sorrows, acquainted with grief"—remained, at some level, a theological abstraction. As educated and socially privileged male theologians in the American ethnic majority, the suffering that Pieper, John Williamson Nevin, and Charles Hodge (not to mention the present authors) experienced was predominately psychological and existential. They never experienced systemic oppression or social marginalization. Perhaps the lack of earthly suffering in the lives of white American theologians in the Reformation traditions helps explain why divine suffering has been relegated to a place of secondary importance in our theology.

The experience of enslaved Africans and their descendants in America differed dramatically. They knew the way of sorrow. They also knew the *Christus dolor*. Their eschatological hope too often had to be deferred; they rarely realized the power of Jesus's victory over evil. Thus in the language of the apostle Paul, they did more than their share on behalf of Christ's body in filling up what is lacking with respect to his afflictions in traditional Christologies (Col. 1:24), and did so in a wide array of oral and written media. Few of them were paid to write or teach about theology. Yet as Dwight Hopkins warrants, they "were radically centered on Jesus," and this is evident

---

of Cullen's African American christological poetry, see especially "The Black Christ," in *On These I Stand: An Anthology of the Best Poems of Countee Cullen* (New York: Harper & Row, 1947), 104–37. See also James H. Smylie, "Countee Cullen's 'The Black Christ,'" *Theology Today* 38 (July 1981): 160–73.

in their sermons, songs, stories, tracts, and memoirs.[2] No one had to explain to them what Paul meant in Philippians by "the sharing of his sufferings" (Phil. 3:10).

Sojourner Truth, Reformed Theology, and the African American Experience

It is worth noting early in this discussion that though African Americans have often articulated the gospel differently, they have not necessarily articulated a different gospel. This is due at least in part to the fact that while Anglo-Americans may not be conversant with black Christology, black Christians have been well versed in traditional Western Christology. This fact is vividly illustrated by the life and work of Sojourner Truth, who represents the intersection of traditional Reformation theology and African American experience.

Sojourner Truth, like Charles Hodge, was born in 1797; she in Hurley, New York, and he in Philadelphia (about 180 miles apart). Their respective life circumstances were obviously very different. Hodge was born into a well-to-do family and raised in a stable Calvinist environment. After he graduated from Princeton Seminary, he studied at a German university and later returned to Princeton to pursue a distinguished career as a theology professor. Truth was born a slave and found freedom at age twenty-nine, eventually devoting her life to the causes of abolition and women's suffrage. She never learned to read or write, but she did dictate memoirs. There are also transcriptions of some of her speeches. For all of their circumstantial differences, however, Charles Hodge and Sojourner Truth had something in common that is significant for our present purposes: they both were shaped in their earliest years by a Reformation—more specifically, an "Amsterdam"—kind of Christianity. They each lived in an environment in which the influence of the kinds of teachings found in the Heidelberg Catechism loomed large.

Hodge obviously knew the Heidelberg Catechism well. While the Westminster Shorter Catechism was the spiritual mainstay of his youth, the Heidelberg has always been a "second catechism"

2. Dwight N. Hopkins, "Slave Theology in the 'Invisible Institution,'" in *Cut Loose Your Stammering Tongue: Black Theology in the Slave Narratives*, 2nd ed. (Louisville: Westminster John Knox, 2003), 15.

in Presbyterian circles, and Hodge quotes it at a number of key points in explaining Calvinist doctrine in his *Systematic Theology*. Truth, for her part, was born into a family of slaves owned by a well-known Dutch Reformed family, and she later served in other Dutch Reformed households. Her native language was Dutch; she spoke no English until she was sold at age nine and spent a brief stint with a family who knew only English. While she eventually identified with a more Wesleyan kind of theology, she likely attended Reformed services in her youth. And we do know, for example, that her oldest daughter, Diana, was a lifelong member of a Dutch Reformed congregation.

Given their shared ecclesiastical background, it should not surprise us that Charles Hodge and Sojourner Truth shared core theological convictions. Each of them strongly affirmed the sovereignty of God, the divine power that brought about the victory of Christ through his incarnation, death on the cross, victorious resurrection, and his ascent to his heavenly throne as the triumphant Ruler. Accounts of her conversations report Truth's affirmation that "God is all in all" and "worketh all in all." Without God's active demonstrations of his mighty power, she was fond of saying, "the waters would not flow, and the fishes could not swim; and all motion must cease." God the Father of Jesus is "to be worshipped at all times and in all places."[3] Likewise Truth affirmed, as Hodge did, the importance of the incarnation of Christ and his willing association with suffering humanity.

But more than Hodge, and along with her fellow slaves and former slaves, Truth emphasized the suffering both of Christ and of God in Christ, as well as Christ's essential identification with the lowly and marginalized. This is very evident in her famous "Ain't I a Woman" speech, a very brief (356-word) oration that she delivered impromptu when she took to the lectern at an 1851 women's suffrage convention in Akron, Ohio. Sternly admonishing her white audience that she too had a woman's voice that deserved a hearing, she spoke of the hardships she had experienced, with a testimony that pointed directly to her confidence that Jesus was in solidarity with her in her sufferings: "I have borne thirteen children and seen most all sold off to slavery, and when I cried out with my mother's grief, none but Jesus heard me."[4]

3. Sojourner Truth, *Narrative of Sojourner Truth*, introduction and notes by Imani Perry (New York: Barnes & Noble Classics, 2005), 78–79.

4. Two versions of Sojourner Truth's speech, "Ain't I a Woman?" (also called "Ar'n't I a Woman?"), come down to us today, one from the *Anti-Slavery Bugle* (June 21, 1851) and

Similarities notwithstanding, the larger perspectives within which Truth and her African American coreligionists, on the one hand, and theologians like Hodge, Nevin, and Pieper, on the other, arranged the two teachings of suffering and triumph is quite different. The theological process went very differently for the African Americans whose Christian beliefs were shaped by the slavery experience. As the well-known "Black Theology" advocate James Cone observed in *The Spirituals and the Blues*, the Christian slaves' reflections on the problem of suffering had little time for the "abstract and universal"; their thinking about God and his purposes moved very quickly to the "concrete,"[5] a theological focus that was spelled out by them in the spiritual songs that they sang. The so-called Negro spirituals of the slavery era gave profound expression to the conviction that Jesus, and only Jesus, understood their suffering because of his own incarnational self-emptying, as in:

> Nobody knows de trouble I see, Lord,
> Nobody knows like Jesus.[6]

And:

> Jesus walked this lonesome valley,
> He had to walk it for himself,
> Nobody else could walk it for him,
> He had to walk it for himself.[7]

Despite the more personal medium, many of the spirituals display a concern for traditional issues important to Reformed and Lutheran theologians. Like their brothers and sisters in the Reformation traditions, African Americans emphasized the danger of sin and the importance of personal conversion:

---

the other from *The Narrative of Sojourner Truth* (1878). Both are accessible in "Sojourner Truth," in *The Norton Anthology of African American Literature*, ed. Henry Louis Gates Jr. and Nellie Y. McKay (New York: Norton, 1997), 196–201. The speech is also available online at http://www.sojournertruth.org/Library/Speeches/AintIAWoman.htm.

5. James H. Cone, *The Spirituals and the Blues: An Interpretation* (Maryknoll, NY: Orbis Books, 1972), 54.

6. "Nobody Knows De Trouble I See," in James Weldon Johnson and J. Rosamond Johnson, *The Books of American Negro Spirituals* (1925–26; New York: Viking, 1940), 1:140–41.

7. On the debate over the origins of this spiritual and the various versions in which it appears, see Eileen M. Johnson, who does identify it as an "African American spiritual" in "Jesus Walked This Lonesome Valley," *Hymn* 57, no. 3 (Summer 2006): 43.

> Somebody's knockin' at yo' do'
> Somebody's knockin' at yo' do'
> O, sinner, why don't you answer?
> Somebody's knockin' at yo' do.'
>
> Knocks like Jesus, Somebody's knockin' at yo' do'
> Knocks like Jesus, Somebody's knockin' at yo' do'
> O, sinner, why don't you answer?
> Somebody's knockin' at yo' do.'[8]

And:

> Sinner, please, don't let dis harves' pass, dis harves' pass.
> Sinner, please, don't let dis harves' pass, harves' pass;
> Sinner, please, don't let dis harves' pass,
> An' die, an lose yo' soul at las' yo' soul at las'.
>
> Sinner, O, see dat cruel tree, see dat cruel tree, Lord!
> Sinner, O, see dat cruel tree, see dat cruel tree, Lord!
> Sinner, O, see dat cruel tree,
> Where Christ has died for you an' me, for you an' me, Lord![9]

The conversion these spirituals call for was not associated with systemic justice or social change, first and foremost. Rather, like other evangelicals, African Americans recognized the necessity of the internal work of God in the individual sinner's heart at conversion:

> You mus' hab dat true religion,
> You mus' hab' yo' soul converted,
> You mus' hab dat true religion,
> You can't cross dere.[10]

Or:

> Lord, I want to be a Christian in-a my heart, in-a my heart,
> Lord, I want to be a Christian in-a my heart.
> I don't want to be like Judas in-a my heart, in-a my heart,
> I don't want to be like Judas in-a my heart. . . .

8. Johnson and Johnson, *Books of American Negro Spirituals*, 1:85–86.
9. Ibid., 2:50–52.
10. Ibid., 100–101.

> Lord, I want to be more holy in-a my heart, in-a my heart,
> Lord, I want to be more holy in-a my heart.
> I just want to be like Jesus in-a my heart, in-a my heart.
> I just want to be like Jesus in-a my heart.[11]

Just as they were for traditional theologians in the European tradition, the themes of personal salvation and holiness were connected for African Americans with recognition of the victory of Jesus over death and the power of God displayed in his resurrection:

> I know dat my redeemer lives, my redeemer lives, Lord!
> I know dat my redeemer lives, my redeemer lives, Lord!
> I know dat my redeemer lives,
> Sinner, please, don't let dis harves' pass, dis harves' pass.

> O, My God is a mighty man o' war, mighty man o' war, Lord!
> My God is a mighty man o' war, mighty man o' war, Lord!
> My God is a mighty man o' war,
> Sinner, please, don't let dis harves' pass, dis harves' pass.[12]

It is important to see these spirituals for what they are. Scholars often downplay (or overlook) the commonalities of African American and evangelical conceptions of sin and salvation because they read all traditional, evangelical language in black spirituals and preaching as code for emancipation. In this way "crossing the Jordan" does not mean entering heaven, but leaving the South; the "gospel train" is not a metaphor for spiritual deliverance, but for temporal deliverance, via literal trains, to black-friendly Northern states. For our purposes, these examples should remind us that in many important ways, black American Christology takes as its starting point central traditional christological commitments. But it moves from there to articulate the kind of *Christus dolor* we seek.

Expanding the Scope of Christ's Sufferings

Consistent as they were with the Reformation traditions' emphasis on sin and salvation, African slaves and their descendants developed and expanded traditional Reformation Christologies in important ways. One way was by expanding the scope of the sufferings of Jesus.

11. Ibid., 72–73.
12. Ibid., 50–52.

Of course they recognized the cross as the epitome of suffering, both human and divine. But unlike the previous theologians we have considered, they believed that the passion of the Christ was not limited to Gethsemane and Golgotha. They were quite comfortable speaking more generally of the suffering of Jesus outside the experience of the cross in the Savior's everyday life. They viewed Jesus as "acquainted with grief" not only because of his passion, but also due to the general conditions of his earthly experience. Thus they felt that Jesus identified with them in his meekness, lowliness, pain, and God-forsakenness. Ill-fated Iola Leroy, the protagonist of a novel by the famous nineteenth-century black writer Frances Harper, asked rhetorically if any knew the Lord as well as black slaves. "Is there . . . a path which we have trodden in this country," she inquired,

> into which Jesus Christ has not put his feet . . . ? Has the negro been poor and homeless? The birds of the air had nests and the foxes had holes, but the Son of man had not where to lay his head. Has our name been a synonym for contempt? "He shall be called a Nazarene." Have we been despised and trodden under foot? Christ was despised and rejected of men. Have we been ignorant and unlearned? It was said of Jesus Christ, "How knoweth this man letters, never having learned?" Have we been beaten and bruised in the prison-house of bondage? "They took Jesus and scourged him." Have we been slaughtered, our bones scattered at the graves' mouth? He was spit upon by the mob, smitten and mocked by the rabble, and died as died Rome's meanest criminal slave.[13]

Because Jesus suffered throughout his life, he was uniquely qualified to comfort and commiserate with oppressed slaves in all aspects of their lives. The real-life prayer of an elderly slave, "Aunt Jane," conveys this sense of identification both pitifully and poignantly. "Dear Massa Jesus," she invoked the Lord of sorrows at a service full of pious slave women,

> we . . . beg Ooner [you] come make us a call dis yere day. We is nutting but poor Etiopian women and people ain't tink much 'bout we. We

13. Frances E. W. Harper, *Iola Leroy, or Shadows Uplifted*, 2nd ed. (1892; College Park, MD: McGrath, 1969), 256. Harper said much the same thing in her own voice in "The Woman's Christian Temperance Union and the Colored Woman," *A. M. E. Church Review* 4 (1888): 313–16. For more on Harper and her work, see Melba Joyce Boyd, *Discarded Legacy: Politics and Poetics in the Life of Frances E. W. Harper, 1825–1911*, African American Life Series (Detroit: Wayne State University Press, 1994).

ain't trust any of dem great high people for come to we church, but do' you is de one great Massa, great too much dan Massa Linkum [the local slave master], you ain't shame to care for we African people.

Come to we, dear Massa Jesus. De sun, he hot too much, de road am dat long and boggy [sandy] and we ain't got no buggy for send and fetch Ooner. But Massa, you 'member how you walked dat hard walk up Calvary and ain't weary but tink about we all dat way. We know you ain't weary for to come to we. We pick out de torns, de prickles, de brier, de back-slidin' and de quarrel and de sin out of you path so day shan't hurt Ooner pierce feet no more.[14]

Women like Frances Harper and Aunt Jane clearly knew what Harriet Jacobs, a fugitive slave herself, referred to simply as "the meek and lowly Jesus."[15]

Such conviction was affirmed constantly by faithful slaves. James Pennington, an ex-slave and Presbyterian pastor, repeated it to bolster faith in those who bore the yoke. In a letter to his family written in 1844, he told his mother, still enslaved, "Mother, dear mother, I know, I feel, mother, the pangs of thy bleeding heart. . . . Thy agonies are by a genuine son-like sympathy mine. . . . But I sincerely hope that with me you bear your agonies to Christ who carries our sorrows."[16] Sister Kelly, a former slave grieving the death of her husband, said, "The devil tried to cheat me, but I jest held on to his [the Lord's] blessed hand. What is written of trouble on the heart is written in his blood."[17]

Christ, and Christ alone, truly understood the slaves. He suffered with them, they believed. In fact, many black Christians said that

14. See Harold A. Carter, *The Prayer Tradition of Black People* (Valley Forge, PA: Judson Press, 1976), 48–49.

15. Harriet A. Jacobs, *Incidents in the Life of a Slave Girl, Written by Herself,* enlarged ed., ed. Jean Fagan Yellin (Cambridge, MA: Harvard University Press, 2000), 67.

16. James W. C. Pennington, *The Fugitive Blacksmith; or, Events in the History of James W. C. Pennington, Pastor of a Presbyterian Church, New York, Formerly a Slave in the State of Maryland, United States* (London: Charles Gilpin, 1849), as included in Yuval Taylor, ed., *I was Born a Slave: An Anthology of Classic Slave Narratives,* vol. 2, *1849–1866,* The Library of Black America (Chicago: Lawrence Hill Books, 1999), 152.

17. Sister Kelly, "Proud of That 'Old Time' Religion," in Milton C. Sernett, ed., *Afro-American Religious History: A Documentary Witness* (Durham, NC: Duke University Press, 1985), 73.

what they called the "lonesome valley" proved to be the best place to fellowship with God.

> My brethuh, want to get religion?
> Go down in de lonesome valley;
> My brethuh, want to get salvation?
> Go down in de lonesome valley,
>
> Go down in de lonesome valley,
> Go down in de lonesome valley, My Lawd,
> Go down in de lonesome valley,
> To meet my Saviuh there.[18]

Or in the words of another song:

> Ef ye want to see Jesus, Go in de wilderness,
> Go in de wilderness, Go in de wilderness,
> Ef ye want to see Jesus, Go in de wilderness
> Leanin' on de Lord.[19]

Christ himself had suffered more than any other single human. He had also suffered righteously, so he knew how to minister to those unjustly treated.

> Nobody knows de trouble I've had,
> Nobody knows but Jesus,
> Nobody knows de trouble I've had,
> Glory hallelu![20]

And like many slaves, Jesus suffered quietly. "He was oppressed, and he was afflicted, yet he did not open his mouth" (Isa. 53:7). So he empathized with slaves who kept from talking back to masters.

18. "Lonesome Valley," in R. Emmet Kennedy, *Mellows: A Chronicle of Unknown Singers* (New York: Albert & Charles Boni, 1925), 98–99.

19. "Ef Ye Want to See Jesus," in *Religious Folk Songs of the Negro, as Sung on the Plantations, new ed . . . from the orig. ed. by Thomas P. Fenner* (Hampton, VA: Institute Press, 1909), 12–13.

20. "Nobody Knows the Trouble I've Had," in William Francis Allen, Charles Pickard Ware, and Lucy McKim Garrison, *Slave Songs of the United States* (New York: A. Simpson, 1867), 55. For the later and more popular rendition of this song, see "Nobody Knows De Trouble I See," in Johnson and Johnson, *Books of American Negro Spirituals*, 1:140–41.

See how they done my Lord
   done my Lord
   done my Lord
See how they done my Lord
An' He never said a mumblin' word.[21]

All this grief and shame Jesus bore willingly as an act of love for, and genuine solidarity with, enslaved Africans. "Jesus have gone to Galilee," as some of the slaves would sing. "I tracked him by his drops of blood, and every drop he dropped in love."[22]

Because they emphasized the suffering of Christ and his compassion, many of the hymns and sermons from black Christians in the era employed the Bible's maternal imagery of God and Jesus, rather than the more masculine, triumphalist imagery preferred by white theologians in the Reformation traditions. John Thompson, a fugitive slave, sang this at a revival shortly after he escaped:

Hark, my soul! it is the Lord;
It is the Saviour, hear his word;
Jesus speaks, he speaks to thee,
He says, poor sinner, love thou me.

I delivered thee when bound,
And when wounded healed thy wound;
Sought thee wandering, set thee right,
Turned thy darkness into light.

Can a woman's tender care
Cease towards the child she bare?
Yes, she may forgetful be,
But I will remember thee.[23]

More famous spirituals, moreover, also used maternal imagery to convey the love of Christ to those who suffered under slavery:

21. "See How They Done My Lord," in Lydia Parrish, *Slave Songs of the Georgia Sea Islands* (New York: Creative Age Press, 1942), 165.

22. *Unwritten History of Slavery: Autobiographical Account of Negro Ex-Slaves*, Social Science Source Documents (Nashville: Social Science Institute, Fisk University, 1945), 24.

23. John Thompson, *The Life of John Thompson, a Fugitive Slave; Containing His History of 25 Years in Bondage, and His Providential Escape* (Worcester, MA: John Thompson, 1856), in Taylor, *I was Born a Slave*, 2:459.

I heard the voice of Jesus callin'
Come unto me and live.
Lie, lie down, weepin' one,
Rest thy head on my breast.
I come to Jesus as I was,
Weary and lone and tired and sad,
I finds in him a restin' place,
And he has made me glad.[24]

Jesus and the Suffering of God

Like Franz Pieper, these preachers, writers, and singers affirm that in Christ God suffered with compassion for the slaves. The suffering Savior had a compassionate Father. The meek and lowly Jesus empathized with the plight of black slaves and cared for them from heaven, and, as one of them remembered decades after manumission, "God lived close to them, too." Another manumitted slave recalled the kindness of the Lord in this way during his boyhood lived in bondage: "When the heart begins to bleed on the inside," he related, "and a child begins to plead with the Master [i.e., the divine Master], I can tell you that something is going to happen. The old slaves didn't know nothing about books, but they did know God. And knowing him they called on him in their trouble and distress, and I can testify that he heard them." Countless slave songs confirmed that God was near in Christ:

He have been wid us, Jesus,
He still wid us, Jesus,
He will be wid us, Jesus,
Be wid us to the end.[25]

---

24. Norman R. Yetman, *Life Under the "Peculiar Institution": Selections from the Slave Narrative Collection* (Huntington, NY: Robert E. Krieger, 1976), 225.

25. Peter Randolph, *From Slave Cabin to Pulpit: The Autobiography of Rev. Peter Randolph: The Southern Question Illustrated and Sketches of Slave Life* (Boston: James H. Earle, 1893), 209; George P. Rawick, ed., *The American Slave: A Composite Autobiography* (Westport, CT: Greenwood Press, 1972–1979), 18:47; Clifton H. Johnson, ed., *God Struck Me Dead: Religious Conversion Experiences and Autobiographies of Ex-Slaves* (Philadelphia: Pilgrim Press, 1969), 70; and "Jesus With Us," as transcribed in Thomas Wentworth Higginson, *Army Life in a Black Regiment and Other Writings*, ed. R. D. Madison (1869; New York: Penguin, 1997), 161.

James Cone has put this starkly: "When the black slave suffered," he has claimed, "God suffered." Jesus himself "was God's Black Slave," in fact, "who had come to put an end to human bondage." But other black Americans have made such claims as well. In the words of Mary Loucks, a nineteenth-century black Methodist, on Calvary "hangs the Deity," the "Godhead" itself "in human flesh."[26]

Professor Howard Thurman often stressed what he described as the "striking similarity between the social position of Jesus . . . and that of the vast majority of American negroes." He employed this similarity in several different ways, both to strengthen black Christians and to criticize conventional, white, Western Christianity. "To those who need profound succor and strength," he suggested, "to enable them to live in the present with dignity,"

> Christianity often has been sterile and of little avail. The conventional Christian word is muffled, confused, and vague. Too often the price exacted by society for security and respectability is that the Christian movement in its formal expression must be on the side of the strong against the weak. This is a matter of tremendous significance, for it reveals to what extent a religion that was born of a people acquainted with persecution and suffering has become the cornerstone of a civilization and of nations whose very position in modern life has too often been secured by a ruthless use of power applied to weak and defenseless peoples.[27]

In a later piece titled "Suffering," Thurman furthered this suggestion. "For many Christians," he explained, "the sense of the presence of the suffering Christ, who in their thought is also the suffering God, makes it possible through his fellowship to abide their own suffering. . . . In his name they can stand anything that life can do to them." Martin Luther King Jr. claimed to be just such a Christian, encouraged by the Lord to stand fast through every hardship. "My personal trials," he wrote, "have . . . taught me the value of unmerited suffering."

> I have lived these last few years with the conviction that unearned suffering is redemptive. There are some who still find the cross a stumbling

26. Cone, *Spirituals and the Blues*, 62, 49; Mary E. Loucks, "The Crucified Saviour," *Star of Zion* 10 (September 10, 1886): 1. For more on God's suffering with the slaves in Christ, see the bibliography at the end of this volume.

27. Howard Thurman, *Jesus and the Disinherited* (Nashville: Abingdon, 1949), 34, 11–12.

block, and others consider it foolishness, but I am more convinced than ever before that it is the power of God unto social and individual salvation. So like the Apostle Paul I can now humbly yet proudly say, "I bear in my body the marks of the Lord Jesus." The suffering and agonizing moments through which I have passed over the last few years have also drawn me closer to God.[28]

Perhaps most famously, James Cone, in *God of the Oppressed* (1975), declared, "The cross of Jesus reveals the extent of God's involvement in the suffering of the weak. He is not merely sympathetic with the social pain of the poor but becomes totally identified with them in their agony and pain. The pain of the oppressed is God's pain," Cone concluded, "for he takes their suffering as his own, thereby freeing them from its ultimate control of their lives." For Cone the black *Christus dolor*, which has long been the quintessential American *Christus dolor*, has now become a global Christ who brings God near to everyone who suffers from oppression.[29]

Identification of Jesus with the Suffering in General

Another way some African American preachers and thinkers moved beyond the traditional categories of Reformation theologians was by generalizing Jesus's identification with black slaves into a principle of Christ's association with all those who were poor, marginalized, or downtrodden. Black Baptist "Rev. Bentley" knew how to drive this doctrine home. During a sermon in Savannah preached in May of 1850, he compared a recent visit of the president of the United States to Jesus, who was present to the lowly all the time. "The president came in a grand, beautiful carriage," Bentley remembered, "and drove to the best house in the whole town. . . . But a cord was drawn around the house to keep us negroes and other poor folks from coming too near. . . . Now, did Christ come in this way?" he asked, appealing to

28. Howard Thurman, "Suffering," in *Disciplines of the Spirit* (Richmond, IN: Friends United Press, 1963), 64–85, reprinted in Anthony B. Pinn, ed., *Moral Evil and Redemptive Suffering: A History of Theodicy in African-American Thought* (Gainesville: University Press of Florida, 2002), 227–45 (quotation from 240); Martin Luther King Jr., "Suffering and Faith," *Christian Century* 77 (27 April 1960): 510.

29. James H. Cone, *God of the Oppressed* (San Francisco: HarperSanFrancisco, 1975), 174–75.

his listeners. "Did He come only to the rich? . . . No! Blessed be the Lord! He came to the poor!" Bentley finished to great applause: "He came to us, and for our sakes, my brothers and sisters. 'Yes, yes! Amen! He came to us! Blessed be His name! Amen! Halleluiah!' responded through the chapel for a good minute or two," as one white witness noted, "and the people stamped with their feet, and laughed and cried, with countenances beaming with joy."[30]

On the basis of this doctrine, many came to understand that to despise the meek and lowly was to hurt the Lord himself and that to love the marginalized was to serve the Lord himself. Indeed, some went so far as to say that God, or Jesus Christ, is black, or nearly so. The black Baptist Silas Floyd asked in a sermon on Thanksgiving Day, 1898, "How may we do something for Christ?" and responded by suggesting that his people serve the needy. As he thought of his "own race," moreover, "despised and rejected of men, a race of sorrows[,] . . . acquainted with grief," he could not help but view it as a surrogate for Christ. Bishop Henry McNeal Turner, a courageous black Methodist, identified his troubled race with God more directly. "God is a Negro," he proclaimed. And when ridiculed in the press, he fired back in *The Voice of Missions* (1898), asserting that black-skinned people "have as much right biblically and otherwise to believe that God is a Negro, as you buckra, or white, people have to believe that God is a fine looking, symmetrical and ornamented white man." W. E. B. Du Bois repeated this theme just five years later. Jesus is "a dark and pierced Jew," he averred. Jesus "was a laborer and black men are laborers; he was poor and we are poor; he was despised of his fellow men and we are despised; he was persecuted and crucified, and we are mobbed and lynched. If Jesus . . . came to America," Du Bois continued forcefully, "he would associate with Negroes and Italians and working people . . . and he would seldom see the interior of the Cathedral of Saint John the Divine."[31] A black Jesus allowed African

30. Adolph B. Benson, ed., *America of the Fifties: Letters of Fredrika Bremer*, Scandinavian Classics (New York: American-Scandinavian Foundation, 1924), 132–33.

31. "Thanksgiving Service," *The Georgia Baptist* 19 (December 1, 1898): 1; Henry McNeal Turner, "God Is a Negro," in *Respect Black: The Writings and Speeches of Henry McNeal Turner*, The American Negro: His History and Literature (New York: Arno Press / *The New York Times*, 1971), 176–77; W. E. B. Du Bois, *The Souls of Black Folk* (1903; New York: Penguin, 1989), 185; and Du Bois, "The Church and the Negro," *Crisis: A Record of the Darker Races* 6 (October 1913): 291. On the association of lynching with the crucifixion of Jesus, see also

Americans to display Christ's identification with their race in their
sufferings and grief.

Reflections

As we close this chapter, we want to suggest three reasons why academic theologians should pay special attention to how the two themes
of *Christus victor* and *Christus dolor* function in the kind of perspective exhibited by Sojourner Truth and other black Christians in
America.

One reason for giving that perspective special attention is simply the
need to sensitize ourselves to the fact that the highly methodological-
systematic approach of a Hodge is not the only way to set forth an
orthodox presentation of biblically based thinking. The christological
systems laid out by Nevin, Pieper, and Hodge relied upon highly tech-
nical language and majored in fine distinctions. It might be tempting
for theologians of similar background to consider this approach more
thoughtful. However, the fact that slaves like Sojourner Truth were
typically illiterate did not mean that they did not engage in careful
theological reflection. The slave spirituals, not to mention the sermons,
letters, and more formal extant literature, are themselves important
embodiments of profound theological insights and need to be taken
seriously as such.

Second, Charles Hodge and Sojourner Truth configure the basic
themes we are exploring here—self-denying suffering and divine
triumphal power—in both similar and different ways, and the two
perspectives can supplement, and even correct, each other theologically. Those of us who care deeply about the task of very carefully
formulated systematic theology and who are committed to a confessional theological tradition will fully expect that Sojourner Truth's
theological insights, if they are to serve the church for the long haul,
protecting Christians from error and equipping them for new challenges, will need to borrow much from a system like Hodge's.[32] At

---

James H. Cone, *The Cross and the Lynching Tree* (Maryknoll, NY: Orbis Books,
2011). For more resources on a dark or black Jesus, see the bibliography at the
end of this volume.

32. While, for example, Sojourner Truth regularly referred to Jesus as God, she
sometimes also seemed to endorse an Arian Christology; see the going back-and-forth
on this in *Narrative*, 50.

the same time, though, it is not insignificant that, unlike Hodge, Sojourner Truth does make much of the lifelong suffering of Christ, rightly reminding us that his atoning work was not restricted to the suffering on Calvary, but that it necessarily showed that "Jesus walked this lonesome valley" throughout his lifetime.

A third reason is closely related to the second. We can identify an important relationship between the very different "social locations" of Charles Hodge and Sojourner Truth and the different ways they configure the two themes in question. Hodge could choose divine power as his theological default position because he himself was a person in power—a respected university professor with considerable social influence. Sojourner Truth's choice of the suffering Jesus as her default position in thinking about the divine nature obviously had something to do with the fact that her own life was marked by consistent suffering and marginalization.

Clearly the nineteenth-century African American context offers an abundance of theological resources for fleshing out the *Christus dolor* theme. And it is important to note that others in that same period also found insight from a black *Christus dolor*. Most significantly, Harriet Beecher Stowe, whose novel *Uncle Tom's Cabin* (1852) was the best-selling book in all of nineteenth-century America (after the Bible, one must add), depicted Christ as black, meek, and lowly several times. "The African race," she opined, "appear as yet to have been companions only of the sufferings of Christ. In the melancholy scene of his death—while Europe in the person of the Roman delivered him unto death, and Asia in the person of the Jew clamoured for his execution—Africa was represented in the person of Simon the Cyrenean, who came patiently bearing after him the load of the cross; and ever since then poor Africa has been toiling on, bearing the wary cross of contempt and oppression after Jesus." Stowe looked forward to the day when "they who suffer with him shall . . . reign," seated on "thrones" and wearing "crowns." However, her tendency to essentialize and romanticize the passive black Christian "Uncle Tom" ought to make us think again about the dangers of a ductile *Christus dolor*. Whites used this stereotype to keep black people down, render them easy, willing martyrs, even justify their lynching. They became the ideal scapegoats for a failing civilization in which saccharine Christian purity and white supremacy required bloody sacrifice. And blacks themselves even took liberties based on the black *Christus dolor* to wage violence in revenge for

their suffering. We turn now to explore the challenges wrapped up
with appropriating a *Christus dolor* theology in the history of the
American South.[33]

33. Harriet Beecher Stowe, preface to *An Autobiography of Josiah Henson (1789–
1876): Harriet Beecher Stowe's "Uncle Tom"* (1877; Mobile, AL: R. E. Publications,
n.d.), 3–4. For Stowe's fictional Uncle Tom, see *Uncle Tom's Cabin; or, Life among
the Lowly,* in *Harriet Beecher Stowe: Three Novels* (New York: Library of America,
1982), 1–519. For Henson's own story, see Josiah Henson, *The Life of Josiah Henson,
Formerly a Slave, Now an Inhabitant of Canada, as Narrated by Himself* (Boston:
Arthur D. Phelps, 1849), in Yuval Taylor, ed., *I Was Born a Slave: An Anthology of
Classic Slave Narratives,* vol. 1, *1770–1849* (Chicago: Lawrence Hill Books, 1999),
719–56. On his role as a model for Stowe's fictional Uncle Tom, see Harriet Beecher
Stowe, *A Key to Uncle Tom's Cabin: Presenting the Original Facts and Documents
upon Which the Story Is Founded; Together with Corroborative Statements Verifying
the Truth of the Work* (Boston: J. P. Jewett, 1853); John Lobb, editorial note to *Autobiography of Josiah Henson,* 5–11; and Robin W. Winks, "The Making of a Fugitive
Slave Narrative: Josiah Henson and Uncle Tom—A Case Study," in *The Slave's Narrative,* ed. Charles T. Davis and Henry Louis Gates Jr. (New York: Oxford University
Press, 1985), 112–46. But note that Stowe's *Christus dolor* was not always black or
male: *Footsteps of the Master* (New York: J. B. Ford, 1877), 265.

6

The Challenge of Application

Christus Dolor *in the American South*

Of the theological resources we have explored to this point, those of the African American tradition seem to be the most promising for those of us who seek a more compassionate Christology. The suffering Messiah that is latent in Lutheran and Reformed dogmatics comes boldly to life in the hymns, sermons, and prayers of subjugated American slaves and their descendants. From these writings emerges an earthy Immanuel—"God with us"—acquainted with the worst of human grief. They make a clear and compelling case that Christ is with us and for us because he has walked—and continues to walk—the path of suffering beside us.

As compelling as the African American Christology of suffering is, it poses challenges for application. Who owns the rights to the crucified Messiah? In the American South after the Civil War, both black and white Christians said that Christ shared their plight. Some envisioned their own suffering as an antitype of Christ's. There are examples of both Anglo- and African American Christians who suffered miserably, unjustly, and patiently, prompting us to agree with their identification with Christ. But there were also whites and blacks who claimed association with Jesus to justify abhorrent sins of racism and violence. This illustrates the need to move beyond the basic principle that Jesus always stands unconditionally on the side of those who suffer.

A Violent *Christus Dolor* in the Anglo-American South

Southern Christians might have become triumphalistic if they had not suffered terrible defeat in the Civil War. In that event, however, Anglo-American Christians in the South preached the *Christus dolor* out of a sense of loss and deep distress. They rarely did so in an effort to defend doctrinal orthodoxy. Neither did they trade in intramural church polemics. But they did look to the past for inspiration in their sorrow. And they proved as ethnocentric as any backward-leaning Lutheran. They are difficult to discuss, for they were racists using Jesus to oppress freed slaves. They employed the *Christus dolor* to solidify and valorize their sense of Southern identity and white supremacy. Examining how they identified with the suffering Messiah can instruct us in the potential of a compassionate Christology for comforting the afflicted in any cultural situation. It also warns us of the dangers of a *Christus dolor* given free rein to validate any and all human passion.

During the past generation, several scholars have discussed the "Lost Cause" of forlorn white Southerners. Some view it as the myth of a lost Southern civilization based on Christian moral values and an agrarian way of life. Others treat it as a Southern Christian form of civil religion that sustained the Southern states during and after Reconstruction. Most employ the term more simply to denote patriotic white nostalgia for the culture of the antebellum South, most visible in rallies for United Confederate Veterans (some of whom survived through the early twentieth century), but also manifest in white support for Jim Crow laws (which lasted through the early 1960s). All of these scholars recognize that Lost Cause rhetoric was often christological, as Southerners interpreted their trauma theologically. As summarized by cultural critic Richard Wightman Fox, the outcome of the war "produced a suffering Jesus who stood for the sacrificial valor of a regional culture. Southerners could construe defeat on the battlefield of war as victory on the battlefield of spirit. Blood sacrifice brought purification, drawing the entire Southern people in their devastation closer to Christ their savior."[1]

1. Richard Wightman Fox, *Jesus in America: Personal Savior, Cultural Hero, National Obsession* (San Francisco: HarperSanFrancisco, 2004), 251. On the religion and

These Southerners, that is, so nearly identified their suffering with the suffering of the Lord that they portrayed the Lost Cause as part of his plan for their redemption—and the suffering of their families as a means of that redemption. According to J. W. Tucker, a Presbyterian pastor, in a sermon preached as hosts of loyal sons of the Confederacy were dying for their country,

> Our cause is sacred. It should ever be so in the eyes of all true men in the South. How can we doubt it, when we know it has been consecrated by a holy baptism of fire and blood. It *has* been rendered glorious by the martyr-like devotion of . . . [those] who have offered their lives as a sacrifice on the altar of their country's freedom.[2]

Many other Confederate clergymen compared their dead to Christ, suggesting that somehow the Lord would wring good—resurrection—from the blood-soaked terrain of their defeated Southern states. At war's end, William Brown, another Presbyterian pastor, exhorted his region's churches,

mythology of the Southern Lost Cause, see Rollin G. Osterweis, *The Myth of the Lost Cause, 1865–1900* (Hamden, CT: Archon Books, 1973), esp. 118–26; Charles Reagan Wilson, *Baptized in Blood: The Religion of the Lost Cause, 1865–1920* (Athens: University of Georgia Press, 1980); Thomas L. Connelly and Barbara L. Bellows, *God and General Longstreet: The Lost Cause and the Southern Mind* (Baton Rouge: Louisiana State University Press, 1982), esp. 12–21; Lewis P. Simpson, "The Southern Republic of Letters and I'll Take My Stand," in *A Band of Prophets: The Vanderbilt Agrarians After Fifty Years* (Baton Rouge: Louisiana State University Press, 1982), 65–91; Gaines M. Foster, *Ghosts of the Confederacy: Defeat, the Lost Cause, and the Emergence of the New South, 1865 to 1913* (New York: Oxford University Press, 1987); William C. Davis, *The Cause Lost: Myths and Realities of the Confederacy*, Modern War Studies (Lawrence: University Press of Kansas, 1996); Gary W. Gallagher and Alan T. Nolan, eds., *The Myth of the Lost Cause and Civil War History* (Bloomington: Indiana University Press, 2000); David W. Blight, *Race and Reunion: The Civil War in American Memory* (Cambridge, MA: Belknap Press of Harvard University Press, 2001), esp. 255–99; David Goldfield, *Still Fighting the Civil War: The American South and Southern History* (Baton Rouge: Louisiana State University Press, 2002); and Arthur Remillard, *Southern Civil Religions: Imagining the Good Society in the Post-Reconstruction Era*, The New Southern Studies (Athens: University of Georgia Press, 2011), 95–103, which presents the Lost Cause as a form of civil religion that was also embodied by Southern white women.

2. J. W. Tucker, "God's Providence in War," in *"God Ordained This War": Sermons on the Sectional Crisis, 1830–1865* (Columbia: University of South Carolina Press, 1991), 236. Tucker preached this sermon in May 1862 to his congregation in Fayetteville, North Carolina. His text was Isaiah 45:7, "I form the light, and create darkness: I make peace, and create evil: I the LORD do all these things" (KJV).

You have been called to pass through deep waters; you have had sorrow upon sorrow. It was the path your Saviour trod and he will grant you in it the comfort of his love and the fellowship of his Spirit. Some of our dear brethren in Christ, and some of them in the ministry, have had cruel mockings and scourgings, have suffered stripes and imprisonments and the loss of all things. . . . Remember, that the church of God has often passed through the heated furnace, but the form of the Son of God has been seen with her and she is still unconsumed.[3]

Southerners continued to think this way about their lost—and Lost Cause—for years to come. In 1897, James Vance preached a sermon at a massive Southern rally honoring Civil War veterans, comparing the Lost Cause to lost causes in the Bible, especially that of Jesus, who achieved something greater through his death than would have been possible without it. "Our ideals survive the hour of defeat," Vance proclaimed. "His enemies could nail Christ to the cross, but they could not quench the ideals he embodied. His seemed to be a lost cause as the darkness fell on the great tragedy at Calvary, but out of what seemed Golgotha's irretrievable defeat has come the cause whose mission it is to save that which is lost." In 1945, historian Kate Coles Donegan related the following anecdote of Father Abram Ryan, a Catholic Civil War chaplain also called the "Southern Bard" and "poet Laureate of the . . . Confederacy":

While visiting his brother's family in Virginia, he arose one morning early and meeting his little niece in the hall he took her in his arms and walked into the dining room. Over the mantel hung a large picture of the Crucifixion and in a very serious manner he asked her if she knew who those wicked men were, that were crucifying Our Saviour? Instantly she replied [*sic*], 'O yes I know," and you can imagine his chagrin when she replied—"The Yankees."[4]

3. Brown is quoted in Henry Alexander White, *Southern Presbyterian Leaders* (New York: Neale, 1911), 347. On this theme, see also Kurt O. Berends, "Confederate Sacrifice and the 'Redemption' of the South," in *Religion in the American South: Protestants and Others in History and Culture*, ed. Beth Barton Schweiger and Donald G. Mathews (Chapel Hill: University of North Carolina Press, 2004), 99–123.

4. "Sermons before the Reunion," *Confederate Veteran* 5 (July 1897): 351; and Kate Coles Donegan, "Personal Reminiscences of Father Ryan," *Alabama Historical Quarterly* 7 (Fall 1945): 450.

Examples abound of this kind of Southern American *Christus dolor*.[5] We mention them not to valorize the racist Lost Cause, but to suggest that there are dangers on the *Via Dolorosa*. The tendency to identify with Jesus in our suffering not only leads at times to what we ought to label rank idolatry: the worship of our families, ethnic groups, and ways of life, but has also been associated—in many times and places—with a strong desire for violent vindication. Many groups have looked to Jesus both for succor in their suffering and for resurrection power—Christian leverage—over others. Indeed, the cruelty perpetrated against black people in the South, as we will see, was also glossed christologically.[6]

A Violent *Christus Dolor* in the African American South

The black *Christus dolor* was not always weak and passive. Stowe's stereotype, in fact, accounts for only a small percentage of the

5. See, for example, Frances Blake Brockenbrough, *A Mother's Parting Words to Her Soldier Boy* (Petersburg, VA: Evangelical Tract Society, n.d.), who encourages her son not to confuse the cause of Christ with that of the armies of the South, like so many others do; the blatantly white supremacist novel written by Henry M. Wharton, a pastor in Virginia, *White Blood: A Story of the South* (New York: Neale, 1906), which does confuse the two (esp. 117–18); Kelly J. Baker, *Gospel According to the Klan: The KKK's Appeal to Protestant America, 1915–1930*, Culture America (Lawrence: University Press of Kansas, 2011), 108–12, which describes the martyrology of the Ku Klux Klan; and Stephen Elliott, *Sermons by the Right Reverend Stephen Elliott, DD, Late Bishop of Georgia; With a Memoir, by Thomas M. Hanckel, Esq.* (New York: Pott & Amery, 1867), the leading Anglican preacher of the Confederacy. Important assessments of Elliott and his providential view of Southern suffering in the war include Edgar Legare Pennington, "Bishop Stephen Elliott and the Confederate Episcopal Church," *The Georgia Review* 4 (April 1950): 233–47; William A. Clebsch, "Stephen Elliott's View of the Civil War," *Historical Magazine of the Protestant Episcopal Church* 31 (March 1962): 7–20; and Dwyn Mounger, "History as Interpreted by Stephen Elliott," *Historical Magazine of the Protestant Episcopal Church* 44 (September 1975): 285–317.

6. It is important to note that other white Southerners living after the Civil War spoke of a rather different Jesus, one who identified with poor folk in every ethnic group, without promoting white supremacy aggressively. Few scholars have paid attention to the folk who loved this Jesus, but see Paul Harvey, *Freedom's Coming: Religious Culture and the Shaping of the South from the Civil War through the Civil Rights Era* (Chapel Hill: University of North Carolina Press, 2005); John Hayes, "Hard, Hard Religion: Faith and Class in the New South" (PhD diss., University of Georgia, 2007), distilled in John Hayes, "Hard, Hard Religion: The Invisible Institution of the New South," *Journal of Southern Religion* 10 (2007), available online at http://jsr.fsu.edu/Volume10/Hayes.pdf; and Erik S. Gellman and Jarod Roll, *The Gospel of the Working Class: Labor's Southern Prophets in New Deal America*, The Working Class in American History (Urbana: University of Illinois Press, 2011).

Christology of suffering in black American history. A stronger, or at least far more resilient, *Christus dolor* has emerged in the development of black theology (as seen in chap. 5). Further, violent and vindictive black men have also appropriated God's incarnate passion, serving as liberating Christ figures for those who bear the yoke and going as far as mass murder in the name of the Redeemer. Their militant *Christus dolor* is a far more sympathetic and attractive Christ figure than its violent white counterparts. The slaves and their descendants needed justice, freedom, and help, which might never have been achieved without a fight. White Americans had fought to win their own independence—from a much less painful tyranny—in their hallowed Revolution. Nevertheless, the common habit of overidentifying with Christ, especially in times of great distress, has done great harm among black Christians in America as well.

Perhaps the best example of this is found in the numerous conspiracies and uprisings of Christian slaves against their white masters. Nearly two hundred and fifty such rebellions have been documented in North American history, each of which involved at least ten black slaves.[7] The best known were led by Gabriel (a.k.a. Gabriel "Prosser," a misnomer) on the outskirts of Richmond (1800),[8] Denmark Vesey in Charleston (1822),[9] and especially Nat Turner, whose

7. See Herbert Aptheker, *American Negro Slave Revolts*, 5th ed. (New York: International Publishers, 1987); Junius P. Rodriguez, ed., *Encyclopedia of Slave Resistance and Rebellion*, 2 vols. (Westport, CT: Greenwood Press, 2007); and, on the most recent literature, Douglas R. Egerton, "African Uprisings," *Reviews in American History* 40 (June 2012): 222–28.

8. For more on Gabriel, see Douglas R. Egerton, *Gabriel's Rebellion: The Virginia Slave Conspiracies of 1800 and 1802* (Chapel Hill: University of North Carolina Press, 1993); James Sidbury, *Ploughshares into Swords: Race, Rebellion, and Identity in Gabriel's Virginia, 1730–1810* (New York: Cambridge University Press, 1997); and Michael L. Nicholls, *Whispers of Rebellion: Narrating Gabriel's Conspiracy*, Carter G. Woodson Institute Series (Charlottesville: University of Virginia Press, 2012).

9. On Vesey's life and work, start with Douglas R. Egerton, *He Shall Go Out Free: The Lives of Denmark Vesey*, rev. ed. (Lanham, MD: Rowman & Littlefield, 2004); David Robertson, *Denmark Vesey: The Buried Story of America's Largest Slave Rebellion and the Man Who Led It* (New York: Alfred A. Knopf, 1999); and John Lofton, *Denmark Vesey's Revolt: The Slave Plot That Lit a Fuse to Fort Sumter* (Kent, OH: Kent State University Press, 1983). On the context of his conspiracy, see also Edward A. Pearson, ed., *Designs against Charleston: The Trial Record of the Denmark Vesey Slave Conspiracy of 1822* (Chapel Hill: University of North Carolina Press, 1998); and James O'Neil Spady, "Power and Confession: On the Credibility of the Earliest Reports of the Denmark Vesey Slave Conspiracy," *William and Mary Quarterly*, 3rd ser., 68 (April 2011): 287–304.

rebellion quickly spread through Southampton County, Virginia, before expiring in the county seat then known as Jerusalem (1831).[10] As James Sidbury has demonstrated, all three of these men had a biblical sense of mission. They were sure that God was with them in their bloody machinations. And "the Bible was central to the conspirators' sense of themselves."[11] Nat Turner even identified himself with Christ and the prophets, tying his own capital punishment to Jesus's crucifixion.

Turner was the son of a runaway slave. Owned by Methodists who allowed him to read and practice Christianity (though under tight restrictions), he was unusually religious from a very young age. Contemporaries described him as a brooding, mystical person. He became a young preacher, undergoing a series of visions that he shared with those around him and that ultimately inspired his rebellion. At the age of thirty-one, on a sultry summer night and into the morning that would follow (August 21–22, 1831), Turner recruited roughly sixty to eighty fellow slave soldiers who, commencing at his own farm, slaughtered every white person they found on the way to Jerusalem—man, woman, and child—with an odd assortment of farming tools and, later, stolen guns. Turner's men killed fifty-seven to sixty people altogether. Local whites soon retaliated, killing scores of blacks. Turner himself was later tried and hanged on an old, gnarled tree that stood in a field outside Jerusalem on November 11, 1831. In the words of Stephen Oates, who has studied the matter extensively, "Nat's secular frustrations and religious visions" created a "storm of black rage that swept

10. On Turner's life and legacy, see Stephen B. Oates, *The Fires of Jubilee: Nat Turner's Fierce Rebellion* (New York: Harper & Row, 1975); Mary Kemp Davis, *Nat Turner Before the Bar of Judgment: Fictional Treatments of the Southampton Slave Insurrection* (Baton Rouge: Louisiana State University Press, 1999); Kenneth S. Greenberg, ed., *Nat Turner: A Slave Rebellion in History and Memory* (New York: Oxford University Press, 2003); and Scot French, *The Rebellious Slave: Nat Turner in American Memory* (Boston: Houghton Mifflin, 2004). On the social context of his rebellion, see also Henry I. Tragle, ed., *The Southampton Slave Revolt of 1831: A Compilation of Source Material* (Amherst: University of Massachusetts Press, 1971); Kenneth S. Greenberg, ed., *The Confessions of Nat Turner and Related Documents* (Boston: Bedford Books of St. Martin's Press, 1996); and Louis P. Masur, *1831: Year of Eclipse* (New York: Hill & Wang, 2001).

11. James Sidbury, "Reading, Revelation, and Rebellion: The Textual Communities of Gabriel, Denmark Vesey, and Nat Turner," in Greenberg, *Nat Turner*, 119–33 (quotation from 122).

across Southampton County and consumed more than 220 lives including Nat's own."[12]

While in prison awaiting sentence, Turner granted a candid interview to a man named Thomas Gray, a racist, skeptical attorney from a slaveholding family who would excoriate Turner's men as "diabolical actors" and denounce Turner himself as "a gloomy fanatic." Gray's transcription of the interview is undeniably biased. Still, it seems to give us Turner's thoughts in Turner's own words.[13]

Turner's thoughts proved to be strikingly christological. He claimed to have been preternaturally spiritual all his life. His friends and family thought him a prophet. Indeed, the Holy Spirit spoke to him on numerous occasions, "which fully confirmed me in the impression that I was ordained for some great purpose in the hands of the Almighty." Turner comported himself accordingly, withdrawing from society whenever he could manage it, devoting himself to prayer, fasting, and other spiritual matters and sharing his messages from God with fellow slaves. "I . . . withdrew myself as much as my situation would permit," he said, "for the avowed purpose of serving the Spirit more fully."

> I sought more than ever to obtain true holiness before the great day of judgment should appear, and then I began to receive the true knowledge of faith. And from the first steps of righteousness until the last, was I made perfect; and the Holy Ghost was with me, and said, "Behold me as I stand in the Heavens"—and I looked and saw the forms of men in different attitudes—and there were lights in the sky . . . [which] were the lights of the Saviour's hands, stretched forth from east to west, even as they were extended on the cross on Calvary for the redemption of sinners. And I wondered greatly at these miracles, and prayed to be informed of a certainty of the meaning thereof—and shortly afterwards, while laboring in the field, I discovered drops of blood on the corn as though it were dew from heaven . . . and I then found on the leaves in the woods hieroglyphic characters, and numbers, with the forms of men in different attitudes, portrayed in blood, and representing the figures I had seen before in the heavens. And now the Holy Ghost

12. Stephen B. Oates, *Our Fiery Trial: Abraham Lincoln, John Brown, and the Civil War Era* (Amherst: University of Massachusetts Press, 1979), 123.

13. Gray interviewed Turner during several meetings held November 1–3, 1831. Within weeks, he published an edited transcription of the interview, *The Confessions of Nat Turner, The Leader of the Late Insurrection in Southampton, Va.* (Baltimore: Lucas & Deaver, 1831), most accessible today in Taylor, *I Was Born a Slave*; quotations from 1:242.

had revealed itself to me, and made plain the miracles it had shown me—For as the blood of Christ had been shed on this earth, and had ascended to heaven for the salvation of sinners, and was now returning to earth again in the form of dew—and as the leaves on the trees bore the impression of the figures I had seen in the heavens, it was plain to me that the Saviour was about to lay down the yoke he had borne for the sins of men, and the great day of judgment was at hand.[14]

That "day of judgment" would involve Turner himself in a starring role. For soon the Spirit appeared again, he said, and told him that "as the Saviour had been baptized so should we [the local slaves] be also." Their masters prohibited them from baptism in church. So "we went down into the water together, in the sight of many who reviled us, and were baptized by the Spirit." Then on May 12, 1828, Turner claimed to hear "a loud noise in the heavens, and the Spirit instantly appeared to me and said the Serpent was loosened, and Christ had laid down the yoke he had borne for the sins of men, and that I should take it on and fight against the Serpent, for the time was fast approaching when the first should be last and the last should be first." Turner began to lay plans for his rebellion three years later. When Gray asked him in his jail cell whether he found himself mistaken about his messianic role now that he faced execution, Turner replied, "Was not Christ crucified"?[15]

As Eric Sundquist has summarized Turner's sense of mission, "In Turner's prophecy slavery is the Antichrist, Revelation is equivalent to revolution, and he is the Redeemer whose acts of chastening, completed by martyrdom, will inaugurate the holy utopia." James Sidbury confirms, "Turner claimed to be the legitimate heir of Christ."[16] We heartily sympathize with Turner's sense of eschatological urgency and condemn the rank injustice he and his fellows clearly suffered. But we also believe that Turner's identification with Christ's sufferings lost its theological footing as it slipped into an association with Christ's role as judge and executioner. As we have seen in this chapter, messianic

14. Taylor, *I Was Born a Slave*, 1:246–48.
15. Ibid., 1:248.
16. Eric J. Sundquist, *To Wake the Nations: Race in the Making of American Literature* (Cambridge, MA: Harvard University Press, 1993), 79; Sidbury, "Reading, Revelation, and Rebellion," 130. On Turner as Christ figure, see also French, *Rebellious Slave*, 189. Cf. Gayraud S. Wilmore, *Black Religion and Black Radicalism: An Interpretation of the Religious History of African Americans*, 3rd ed. (Maryknoll, NY: Orbis Books, 1998), 90.

complexes—whether white or black—can descend into violence when not properly limited by theological rules.

A Continuing Challenge

The tendency to identify with Christ in our sufferings—or, more dangerously, to identify Christ with our sufferings—is one that tempts Christians of nearly all racial and ethnic groups, in nearly every time and place. And though white-black christological differences in America were expressed most forcefully in the tragic era of slavery, Reconstruction, and Jim Crow, this tendency, racialized or not, has recurred in numerous other times and places in American church history. Jonathan Ebel dedicates an entire chapter in his book to treating the ways in which the suffering and death of soldiers in the First World War was interpreted christologically and redemptively. "Americans involved in the Great War were certainly capable of seeing the obliterated bodies of those killed in war and of thinking their lives wasted," Ebel writes, "but most saw something else. They looked upon twisted or still-writhing bodies as meaningful sacrifices, whether on the altar of a righteous cause or a neighboring altar of heroic selflessness. Pilots who fell from the sky were martyrs. Soldiers, bleeding, broken, and dead, were imitators of Christ."[17]

As such appropriations of Christ and his suffering demonstrate, a freewheeling exploitation of the *Christus dolor* is dangerous. Regulations are needed if we are to steer the ship of christological reflection in a salutary and orthodox direction. Such regulations needn't nullify our rightful claims to Christ, the God-man who empathizes with our weakness and distress and knows our sorrow, pain, and suffering. Like the best representatives in American history show us, we can and should embrace the *Christus dolor*, seeking to establish and live out of a more compassionate Christology. But to do so most productively, we need some common rules. We need guidance from the Bible and our doctrinal traditions. In the conclusion, we invite you to consider this matter with us as we offer some suggestions for those who want to work with us toward a more global and compassionate Christology.

17. Jonathan H. Ebel, *Faith in the Fight: Religion and the American Soldier in the Great War* (Princeton: Princeton University Press, 2010), 76–77.

Conclusion

The American *Christus dolor* has a long and hallowed history, dating back at least to the antebellum period.[1] Although never a leading feature of American Christology, the Christ of sorrows has appeared frequently and powerfully in the writings, songs, and piety of many of our people. It is true that he has not comported well with the chronic cheerfulness and cockiness of mainstream America. Many of the disciples of Jesus have exploited his divinity for self-serving ends, overidentifying with him in their sorrow and distress (and forgetting, hypocritically, that Christ did not regard his own equality with God as a thing "to be exploited," Phil. 2:6). Indeed, American history shows us that we often fashion the kind of Christ we need—or think we need—whether we find ourselves in power or in weakness and despair. Still, the *Christus dolor* has served the needs of many who suffer with him in the shadows or on the margins of American social history, and their testimonies to Christ's suffering-with provide a corrective to more mainstream American Christologies.

In this conclusion, then, we want to offer three words of encouragement for those who seek a more global and compassionate Christology. First, we make the simple point that theological constructs are often expressed somewhat differently in different social contexts—even by

---

1. For intimations of this Jesus in the work of English Puritans in colonial America, see Stephen J. Nichols, *Jesus Made in America: A Cultural History from the Puritans to "The Passion of the Christ"* (Downers Grove, IL: IVP Academic, 2008), 19–45.

those who agree in basic theological principles. Second, we reiterate that Jesus is unique, God's one and only Son, the promised Savior of the world, and that while Christians are united with him and bear his name in the world, we need to avoid the common tendency to see him in all who suffer or to lapse into a messianic complex. Third, we describe how we believe the *Christus victor* and *Christus dolor* themes can coexist, building on earlier chapters to construct a more comprehensive Christology.

A Shared Theology in Diverse Social Locations

As we have seen, the way of arranging specific Christian themes in a larger perspective—the sort, for example, that might be spelled out in a catechism—will differ for various social locations within the Christian community. Staying briefly with the experience of African Americans shaped by the slavery experience, Sojourner Truth's younger contemporary, Frederick Douglass, was also a former slave, and in 1848 he wrote a letter to his former owner, in which he described their relationship in explicitly theological terms: "You are a man," he wrote, "and so am I. God created both, and made us separate beings. I am not by nature bound to you, or you to me."[2] Like Sojourner Truth, Douglass saw himself as a free creature who belonged to his Creator—a fact that nullified any human claim of "ownership" or "belonging." What counts as "self-denial" in Douglass's view of his relationship to God is also a profound basis for a strong self-affirmation as he responded to the claims of the human slave-"owner." And the God to whom he belonged in his creaturehood was the one who thoroughly understood his human journey because of the incarnational ministry of Jesus Christ.

If either Sojourner Truth or Frederick Douglass, then, had produced a catechism, it is unlikely that they would have come up with a better opening question-and-answer to express what they wanted to say in the context of a slavery culture than the Heidelberg's own first answer: "That I, with body and soul, both in life and in death, am not my own, but belong to my faithful Savior Jesus Christ." The

2. Frederick Douglass, "Letter to Thomas Auld," September 3, 1848, in *Frederick Douglass: Selected Speeches and Writings*, ed. Philip Foner, abridged and adapted by Yuval Taylor, The Library of Black America (Chicago: Lawrence Hill Books, 1999), 113. Also available online at http://www.yale.edu/glc/archive/1121.htm.

insistence that one belongs to Christ is a profound challenge to the reality that the American slavery system presupposed.

Of course, Charles Hodge would also make the affirmation of belonging to Christ a very basic theme in his understanding of the faith. But like the belief in Christ's earthly suffering that Hodge shared with the Christian slaves, such an affirmation may function differently in his case, standing in relationship to other beliefs in different configurations than in Sojourner Truth's understanding of those same themes.

In spite of these different configurations, however, there certainly is a shared core meaning in the ways both perspectives understand selfhood. In a fundamental sense, the Christian slave's understanding of what it means to belong to Jesus is not totally different from the understanding of selfhood held by a Christian who writes volumes of dogmatics. The way that core conviction functions in the lives of each will certainly be colored by their different social locations, as well as in how the conviction gets nuanced in relation to other key themes within each person's theological perspective. But what we want to highlight here is that as Christians face widely diverse circumstances, which require different emphases in the way they configure theology, they can—and should—nonetheless express a shared theology that unites them in the body of Christ. And our exploration of the *Christus dolor* theme in this book aims to understand better both the commonness and the relevance of diverse life situations.

The Uniqueness of Jesus's Sufferings

While we have observed the tremendous value of appropriating a theology of Christ as our cosufferer, we have also noted the danger of misapplying the *Christus dolor* when disconnecting it from orthodox Christian theology and identifying Christ with anyone who suffers. Steve Stein, for example, describes the ways in which the early Shakers identified the sufferings and persecution of Mother Ann Lee with the sufferings and persecution of Christ on behalf of the world, using this identification to buttress their claim that Lee was the female Christ figure—or the female version of Christ, or the female coming of Christ.[3]

3. Stephen J. Stein, "Celebrating and Sacralizing Violence: Testimonies Concerning Ann Lee and the Early Shakers," *American Communal Societies Quarterly* 3 (January 2009): 3–12.

In a more recent example, Scott Hoffman addresses the popular reception of the murder of Matthew Shepard, the twenty-one-year-old University of Wyoming student lured to his death in a homophobic hate crime on October 12, 1998. Hoffman shows that many Americans have deemed, and proclaimed, Matthew Shepard to be a gay martyr, a Christ figure who suffered on behalf of his people and won a martyr's reward in heaven. Hoffman interprets Shepard's "martyrdom" in relation to the history of well-known martyrdoms of oppressed American minorities, particularly the lynchings and murders of African Americans such as Emmett Till and Martin Luther King Jr.[4]

Matthew Shepard was indeed subjected to horrifying torture. His death is a vivid example of cruel suffering at the hands of people who inflict terrible evils on their fellow human beings. Viewed theologically, however, the Shepard hagiography is an example of the ongoing tendency to co-opt the passion of Jesus for our own political purposes. Many such purposes are good, and ought to be supported, but not by politicizing the atoning death of Christ to gain sociocultural power. Indeed, the stories of both Mother Ann Lee and Matthew Shepard provide examples of people seeking christological leverage in the midst of violent suffering that cannot be linked to the suffering of Christ without some important theological nuancing.

One of the lessons to be learned from the diverse American tale we've explored in this volume is that disciples ought to identify with Jesus in his suffering while recalling what the Anglican theologian Graham Tomlin has affirmed of its "uniqueness." In our efforts to develop a truly global, comprehensive, and compassionate Christology, we need to check our tendency to overcontextualize, using Christ to suit ourselves and gain power over others. "The word of the cross is unique," as Tomlin has reminded us. "It will not allow Christians to impose their faith . . . on others," but waits "for its truth to be recognized, suffering misunderstanding and disdain." Our world is "justifiably nervous that absolute truths are inherently . . . oppressive." But cruciform faith "offers an absolute Truth," the Lord of sorrows in the flesh, and this Truth "by its very nature denies coercion as a way to assert itself. Instead, it offers and forms a community dedicated

4. Scott W. Hoffman, "'Last Night, I Prayed to Matthew': Matthew Shepard, Homosexuality, and Popular Martyrdom in Contemporary America," *Religion and American Culture: A Journal of Interpretation* 21 (Winter 2011): 121–64.

to learning ways of love for enemies, forgiveness and hospitality to the 'other.'"[5]

Our tendency as Christians is to validate our projects on behalf of those in need—no matter how far removed from the witness of the Scriptures—by conjoining them with Christ, giving them theological power. There is a fine line between a salutary solidarity with Jesus in his suffering and a presumptuous co-opting of that suffering for ourselves. If American history teaches anything about Christology and its social implications, it warns us of the dangers—for the privileged and the oppressed—of succumbing to a messianic complex. The *Via Dolorosa* does lead to eternal life. It offers resurrection power. But those who travel it must follow Jesus through the "lonesome valley," participating—patiently, compassionately, selflessly—in God's redemptive suffering for the world.

A Global *Christus Dolor*

Just before the conclusion of the last session, in 1965, of the momentous Second Vatican Council, the gathered Catholic bishops adopted a document to which they gave the title "Pastoral Constitution on the Church in the Modern World." The document is more commonly referred to as *Gaudium et Spes*, Latin for the first words of the document's oft-quoted opening sentences:

> The joys and the hopes, the griefs and the anxieties of the [human beings] of this age, especially those who are poor or in any way afflicted, these are the joys and hopes, the griefs and anxieties of the followers of Christ. Indeed, nothing genuinely human fails to raise an echo in their hearts.[6]

That bold affirmation that "nothing genuinely human fails to raise an echo" captures a key emphasis of what we have been arguing in these pages. A compassionate Christology must be grounded in a profound conviction that the Son of God understands the deepest hopes and fears of the human condition. And the bishops not only

---

5. Graham Tomlin, "The Uniqueness of Christ's Suffering and Death on the Cross," in *Christ the One and Only: A Global Affirmation of the Uniqueness of Jesus Christ*, ed. Sung Wook Chung (Milton Keynes, UK: Paternoster, 2005), 61–62.

6. *Gaudium et Spes*, 1, at: http://www.vatican.va/archive/hist_councils/ii_vatican _council/documents/vat-ii_cons_19651207_gaudium-et-spes_en.html.

affirmed this but also provided an elaborate rationale for their affir-mation. At the core of their rationale, however, was the reality of the incarnational ministry of the Son of God. "Only in the mystery of the incarnate Word," the bishops wrote, "does the mystery of man take on light," because in his incarnation Jesus "worked with human hands, He thought with a human mind, acted by human choice and loved with a human heart. Born of the Virgin Mary, he has truly been made one of us, like us in all things except sin."[7]

Popular evangelical piety also affirms the Son of God's empathic grasp of the realities of our human condition, an affirmation that comes across clearly, for example, in the familiar words of Joseph Scriven's "What a Friend We Have in Jesus":

> Have we trials and temptations?
> Is there trouble anywhere?
> We should never be discouraged—
> Take it to the Lord in prayer.
> Can we find a friend so faithful,
> Who will all our sorrows share?
> Jesus knows our every weakness;
> Take it to the Lord in prayer.

What does not come through clearly, however, is the theological basis for this profound testimony that "Jesus knows our every weak-ness." Except for the explicit reference to Jesus, Scriven could be relying, in affirming the divine compassion for us in our frailty, solely on the Old Testament's assurance that the Creator has intimate knowl-edge of the human nature that he has designed. And that surely is a source of much legitimate comfort for those who might otherwise despair that they are alone in their "trials and temptations." But—as we have been arguing in these pages—there is more, much more. The New Testament itself offers us the firm basis for our confidence in a Savior who "knows our every weakness." We can "approach the throne of grace with boldness" precisely because "we do not have a high priest who is unable to sympathize with our weaknesses, but we have one who in every respect has been tested as we are, yet without sin" (Heb. 4:15–16).

We wrote this book, not because evangelicals need to be reminded that they do have "a friend in Jesus," but because that deep conviction

7. *Gaudium et Spes*, 22.

needs more explicit theological reinforcement. And, as we said by way of launching this discussion, it was our encounter with our Japanese friends that convinced us that this reinforcement was much needed. We love evangelical piety; it has been for both of us an important gift from the Lord in our personal lives. But a piety that is not grounded in a theology that is clear about the connection between what we feel and what we do can go awry.

Our Japanese Christian friends are quick to admit their indebtedness to Anglo-American missionaries who pointed them to the good news that God has a Savior who entered into our human condition to bear the sins and griefs of persons from every tribe and nation. Yet our Japanese friends are also rightly critical of a theological portrayal of Jesus—one that often looms large in the very communities that nurtured the missionary movement—as a "manly" Christ whose redemptive mission is spelled out in triumphalist terms. To be sure, evangelical theology has also attended much to the suffering of the Son of God; but the portrayals of that suffering, as we have seen, often focus primarily on the unique agonies of the cross. The Jesus of much of our explicit theology has often been a Savior who suffers *for* us, but not *with* us.

Our task here, then, has been to make the theological case for a compassionate Christology that does justice to our awareness, so clear in our evangelical piety, of the Savior's empathic solidarity with us in our human trials and temptations. Furthermore, we have taken pains to insist that none of this requires a downplaying of the unique dimensions of Christ's redemptive suffering that have always figured so prominently in evangelical theological scholarship.

To recognize that Jesus has suffered *with* us needs in no way to detract from the fact that in eternally significant ways he also suffered *for* us. Without the once-for-all transaction on Calvary, where he bore the full burden of our sin and guilt in ways that we could never do for ourselves, we are lost. But, and this is what we have endeavored to highlight in these pages, it is a good thing to be clear about the path—including the lonesome valleys—that he had to walk on the very human journey that began in Bethlehem's stable.

Christus Victor
and *Christus Dolor*

An Afterword

Willie James Jennings

There is a revolution taking place in Christian theology. It is a revolution that Christian theology itself is yet to articulate fully. The elements of this revolution are being spied out, one by one. The first crucial element of this revolution is the growing clarity and power of the designation "global Christianity." Another element is the effects of various conceptualities—postevangelical, postcolonial, even the almost exhausted postmodern—on theology. Another crucial element is the increased volume of formerly colonized subaltern theological voices who now present multigenerational Christian reflection shaped in the crucible of white Western supremacy and white masculine intellectual hegemony. Last there is the coming demographic shifts that will transform majority (read: white) culture into minority (read: other) culture. Together these changes constitute a fundamentally new condition for doing theology.

Indeed, we have reached a crucial moment in the discursive practice called theology. As we enter this time of revolution, Christian theology finds itself caught in endless self-presentation. Theologians are increasingly producing basic texts of theology and publishers are feverishly putting out introductions to theology, or companions to theology, or dictionaries of theology as though the crucial need is to reintroduce Christian thought and its systems of reflection. We could follow some common narratives being proposed today, which see this moment of endless, even obsessive self-presentation as the final outworkings of a post-Christendom moment. Some suggest that we respond to this new situation by reasserting the grammar of the faith, and invite Christians to enter more deeply into the logics of their theological traditions.

This moment, however, is not one in which people in the academy or in churches are unable to define or understand Christian theology or their traditions. The problem at this moment is with theology's placement, theology's deployment, which presses on us the question, Where do you put theology now?

Where do you put theology in relation to educational systems and programs of intellectual formation? Where do you put it in relationship to the presentation of other religious systems of thought? Where do you put it in relation to other disciplinary discursive practices, like sociology or economics? Where do you put it in relation to other ecclesial practices, especially spiritual disciplines? Where do you put it in relation to strategies of political or social intervention, or cultural or religious collaboration, or engagement with scientific investigations? These are not questions about the value, confidence, or reach of theology. These questions have to do with the position of theology in relation to its movement *away from* its historic pedagogical foundationalism.

With the emergence of colonialism Christian theology enjoyed the benefits of a pedagogical foundationalism in Western educational programs both in the metropolis and in the colony through which its reason for existence was self-evident and in no real need of justification. There was no need to outline its connection to political economies or social systems. Christian theology was at the center of the civilizing impulse that established doctrine and Bible knowledge as a fundamental basis on which to build Western educational systems and proper intellectual formation. Such a hegemonic place for theology allowed theologians to imagine *an imperial position of adjudication for theology itself.*

Christian theology emerged out of the perennial need to give an account of the basic realities of Christian existence, to present the doctrines of the faith, and to teach people what Christians have believed and should believe. This perennial need dovetails with the question of theology's placement precisely because *what* should be taught is part of the architecture of *how, when, where, and to whom* it should be taught. But this is not a simple matter of logistics. The position of theology deeply shapes its performance. Theology is about a process of education in which people are invited into a way of discernment and of making judgments about faithful Christian life and faithful Christian thinking about life. Yet the questions that have been opened up in this moment are, From where does one make those judgments? and, Who is making those judgments? The loss of Christian theology's hegemonic position within Western educational systems and the collapse of the civilizing impulse within which theology enjoyed an imperial right of adjudication means that the position of theological judgment has now come into view as never before.

Clearly, all across the United States and in other parts of the world, there are some who are working very hard to restore Christian theology to its pedagogical foundationalist position through the explosion of Christian K–12 educational programs. Regardless of the merits or demerits of such efforts, the question of position remains and with it the recognition of a new situation for all those who wish to speak theologically. The questions of who is speaking and from where they speak are now being pressed into the work of theology. Yet these questions are far more than prolegomena. Nor can they be reduced to concerns about theological method or context. The situation these questions expose is the inescapable demand for theologians to make explicit their quest to think themselves through their work of theological adjudication.

This remarkable text by Mouw and Sweeney marks an extraordinary moment in evangelical theological reflection. This kind of reflection would have been unthinkable even twenty-five years ago. Here we have a text that takes Asian (Japanese) and African American theological voices seriously and recommends such theological voices and concerns as crucial to *responsible* christological reflection today. Although their engagement with contemporary Asian and African American voices is not as robust as we would wish, Mouw and Sweeney establish a clear point—these voices must be taken seriously as crucial interlocutors in thinking the possibility of a helpful Christology at this moment.

The authors have entered into a vital question: What is the relation of Christ's suffering to the suffering of peoples? They have also been pushed into this place by the new situation of theology. The voices

of so many Christians are now being heard in their identification of
the wounds of Christ with their wounds. So these authors engage this
question, drawing on Reformed and Lutheran theological sensibilities
regarding the divine and human natures of Christ, the significance of
Christ's suffering, and the ongoing placement of his body in relation
to the bruising of other bodies. In all these things we see two beautiful theological minds working. They move us through the works
of Nevin, Pieper, and Hodge, showing us the continuing power of
their ideas and their doctrinal significance. What is more revealing
is the subtlety with which they situate the christological reflection of
each writer within their particular cultural framework. The authors
clearly recognize that the angles of concern that form the Christology
of each writer are constituted by much more than the articulation
of orthodoxy. The authors, in this regard, are acknowledging a level of
position that gestures toward our new moment.

The most revealing point of this text, however, exposes the continuing struggle of theology to fully enter our new moment. In chapter 6,
our authors pose the following question in relation to black suffering
in America (and more generally the suffering of peoples within the
colonialist matrix): "As compelling as the African American Christology of suffering is, it poses challenges for application. *Who owns
the rights to the crucified messiah?* In the American South after the
Civil War, both black and white Christians said that Christ shared
their plight" (emphasis added).

This is a disappointing question. It not only plays in a trope of
commodification, even reification, but it tries to connect what is impos-
sible to join together, commodity of form and the suffering of Jesus
of Nazareth. Ultimately, this could be seen as simply a throwaway
line that points to the real challenge of outlining processes of christological identification. Yet such a statement is possible only under the
conditions of penal substitutionary visions of the atonement (what
Christ did for us) joined to real narratives of suffering by Christians
reduced simply to proprietary claims (even complaints) that must be
adjudicated. The trope imagines a judge listening to these complaints.
It reflects a position for theology that is a complete illusion.

It is, however, a position that ushers back to the colonialist order
of things when, under the various European civilizing operations,
theology was a hegemonic, discursive practice fully engaged in the
formation of white subjectivity, even in the bodies of nonwhite subjects. The turn in the text at this point to matters of adjudication is

characteristic of two abiding problems in theology, both of which reflect the lack of a sufficiently historical (theological) consciousness.

The first problem shows itself in the authors' treatment of their exemplars. Each of the Christologies presented is captured in the problems of supersessionism with its concomitant failures to draw consequential or decisive import from the Jewishness of Jesus, the significance of his people, and the gentiles. African American voices mentioned in the text gesture toward these matters, but the authors do not seize on this possibility.

It would be unfair to imagine the exemplars or even our authors to have been able to press into the inner logics of the body of Jesus in relation to his people and its implications for gentile existence. However, the new moment now thrust on theology makes such a bypass profoundly disabling of christological reflection on suffering that wishes to aid the church at risk in a world capitalist system—a system that is able to mobilize narratives and identities of victimization to bolster its own invitations to agency fully within practices of consumption. It is by pressing deeply into the inner logic of the Jewishness of Jesus that we move to a different position from which to grasp the pedagogy of listening to suffering flesh. This would absolutely dissolve the question the authors posed at such a critical moment in this text. It would not, however, completely resolve the challenge of thinking through processes of christological identification.

The necessary crucial step to think through these processes brings us to the second abiding problem in theology, which is its failures of narration. It is now necessary for theology, especially in North America, to enter strategically into historical accounts that take seriously the transformations of the world with the advent of the colonialist moment. Such historical accounts move us beyond simple narratives of victims and oppressors and toward the ways in which victimization is woven inside the formations of subjects and subjectivities. Colonialism fostered the fashioning of life strategies with and against terror, within economies of pleasure, and bound them to racial and gender formation, which yielded and still yields life narratives in reciprocal relationship. This means that narratives of suffering do not first require adjudication but analyses of their interplay as constitutive elements in the creation of the modern racial world and racial subjects.

How any suffering people claim the cosuffering of Jesus is not a matter of falsification or authentication; rather, it is about how they narrate their history in relation to the history of the suffering of the

Jewish Jesus and the new people, both Jew and gentile, constituted in his body. This is not a matter of historical comparison but of grasping the new identity that emerges out of life with Jesus and the powerful new direction our life must take in obedience to him. This means that any and every identification with the suffering Jesus carries within it the dangerous memory of the joining of peoples who hate each other, kill each other, and in truth have realized that they have no hope unless they learn to love each other through him. Jesus draws us toward the suffering of others, to listen carefully to their anguish, and at the very least to understand their desire for identification. Such a desire is (even if weak) turned in the direction of that new community that makes possible the new identity that announces the real victory of Christ.

The crucial question that this landmark text presses on us is this: Now that we are being pressed to reckon with the complicated history of both Christianity's service to those who suffer and its support (and sometimes instigation) of suffering, how do we engage in responsible christological reflection? The answer to that question will be found just as much in how we position our bodies in relation to the body of Jesus as in the particular doctrinal angles we articulate as essential to maintaining a robust Christology.

Resources for Christological Reflection from Our Japanese and African American Interlocutors

Many of our sources can be found in the notes above. For those who would like to think with us about the issues we have raised, we offer this summary bibliography of our English-language sources.

On Modern Japanese Church History and Theology in General

Chua, How Chuang. "Japanese Perspectives on the Death of Christ: A Study in Contextualized Christology." PhD diss., Trinity Evangelical Divinity School, 2007.

Drummond, Richard Henry. *A History of Christianity in Japan*. Christian World Mission Books. Grand Rapids: Eerdmans, 1971.

Furuya, Yasuo, ed. *A History of Japanese Theology*. Grand Rapids: Eerdmans, 1997.

Inagaki, Hisakazu, and J. Nelson Jennings. *Philosophical Theology and East-West Dialogue*. Currents of Encounter: Studies on the Contact between Christianity and Other Religions, Beliefs, and Cultures. Amsterdam: Rodopi, 2000.

Jennings, J. Nelson. *Theology in Japan: Takakura Tokutaro (1885–1934)*. Lanham, MD: University Press of America, 2005.

Koyama, Kosuke. *Mount Fuji and Mount Sinai: A Critique of Idols.* Maryknoll, NY: Orbis Books, 1985.

Lee, Samuel. *Rediscovering Japan, Reintroducing Christendom: Two Thousand Years of Christian History in Japan.* Lanham, MD: Hamilton Books, 2010.

Maruyama, Tadataka. "The Cross and the Cherry Blossom: The Gospel and Japanese Culture at a Crossroads." *Trinity Journal* 21 (Spring 2000): 45–60.

Michalson, Carl. *Japanese Contributions to Christian Theology.* Philadelphia: Westminster, 1960.

Miyahira, Nozomu. "Christian Theology under Feudalism, Nationalism and Democracy in Japan." In *Christian Theology in Asia*, edited by Sebastian C. H. Kim, 109–28. Cambridge: Cambridge University Press, 2008.

Orevillo-Montenegro, Muriel. *The Jesus of Asian Women.* Women from the Margins. Maryknoll, NY: Orbis Books, 2006.

Uchimura, Kanzō. *The Complete Works of Kanzō Uchimura.* 7 vols. Tokyo: Kyobunkwan, 1971–73.

Yagi, Seiichi. "The Dependence of Japanese Theology upon the Occident." *Japan Christian Quarterly* 30 (October 1964): 258–61.

Yamamoto, Kanō. "Theology in Japan: Main Trends of Our Time." *Japan Christian Quarterly* 32 (January 1966): 37–47.

Yewangoe, A. A. Theologia Crucis *in Asia: Asian Christian Views on Suffering in the Face of Overwhelming Poverty and Multifaceted Religiosity in Asia.* Amsterdam Studies in Theology. Amsterdam: Rodopi, 1987.

On the Roman Catholic Novelist Shusaku Endo

Bussie, Jacqueline A. "Believing Apostates: Laughter in Shusaku Endo's *Silence*." Chap. 4 in *The Laughter of the Oppressed: Ethical and Theological Resistance in Wiesel, Morrison, and Endo.* New York: T&T Clark, 2007.

Endo, Shusaku. *Deep River.* Translated by Van C. Gessel. New York: New Directions, 1994.

———. *A Life of Jesus.* Translated by Richard A. Schuchert. 1973. Reprint, New York: Paulist Press, 1978.

———. "Mothers." In *Stained Glass Elegies: Stories by Shusaku Endo*, edited and translated by Van C. Gessel, 108–35. New York: New Directions, 1984.

———. *Silence.* Translated by William Johnston. New York: Taplinger, 1969.

———. *The Samurai.* Translated by Van C. Gessel. New York: New Directions, 1982.

Gessel, Van C. "Voices in the Wilderness: Japanese Christian Authors." *Monumenta Nipponica* 37 (1982): 437–57.

————. "Salvation of the Weak: Endō Shūsaku." Chap. 6 in *The Sting of Life: Four Contemporary Japanese Novelists*. New York: Columbia University Press, 1989.

Mase-Hasegawa, Emi. *Christ in Japanese Culture: Theological Themes in Shusaku Endo's Literary Works*. Brill's Japanese Studies Library. Leiden: Brill, 2008.

Netland, John T. "Encountering Christ in Shusaku Endo's Mudswamp of Japan." In *Historicizing Christian Encounters with the Other*, edited by John C. Hawley, 166–81. Basingstoke, UK: Macmillan, 1998.

Williams, Mark B. *Endō Shūsaku: A Literature of Reconciliation*. The Nissan Institute/Routledge Japanese Studies Series. London: Routledge, 1999.

On the Lutheran Theologian Kazoh Kitamori

Kitamori, Kazō. "Is 'Japanese Theology' Possible?" *Northeast Asia Journal of Theology* 3 (September 1969): 76–87.

————. "The Japanese Mentality and Christianity." *Japan Christian Quarterly* 26 (July 1960): 167–74.

————. "The Problem of Pain in Christology." In *Christ and the Younger Churches: Theological Contributions from Asia, Africa, and Latin America*, edited by Georg F. Vicecom, 83–90. London: SPCK, 1972.

Kitamori, Kazoh. *Theology of the Pain of God: The First Original Theology from Japan*. 1946. Reprint, Richmond, VA: John Knox, 1965.

————. "The Theology of the Pain of God." *The Japan Christian Quarterly* 19 (Autumn 1953): 318–20.

McWilliams, Warren. "Kazoh Kitamori: The Pain of God." In *The Passion of God: Divine Suffering in Contemporary Protestant Theology*. Macon, GA: Mercer University Press, 1985.

Meyer, Richard. "Toward a Japanese Theology: Kitamori's Theology of the Pain of God." *Concordia Theological Monthly* 33 (May 1962): 261–72.

Mutoh, Kazuo. "Kitamorian Theology." *The Japan Christian Quarterly* 19 (Autumn 1953): 321–24.

Christological Reflection on God's Suffering with Slaves and Lynching Victims

Allen, William Francis, Charles Pickard Ware, and Lucy McKim Garrison. *Slave Songs of the United States*. New York: A. Simpson, 1867.

Berends, Kurt O. "Confederate Sacrifice and the 'Redemption' of the South." In *Religion in the American South: Protestants and Others in History and Culture*, edited by Beth Barton Schweiger and Donald G. Mathews, 99–123. Chapel Hill: University of North Carolina Press, 2004.

Carter, Harold A. *The Prayer Tradition of Black People*. Valley Forge, PA: Judson Press, 1976.

Carter, J. Kameron. *Race: A Theological Account*. New York: Oxford University Press, 2008. See esp. 293–312.

Cone, James H. *The Cross and the Lynching Tree*. Maryknoll, NY: Orbis Books, 2011.

———. *God of the Oppressed*. San Francisco: HarperSanFrancisco, 1975.

———. *The Spirituals and the Blues: An Interpretation*. Maryknoll, NY: Orbis Books, 1972.

Cullen, Countee P. "The Black Christ." In *On These I Stand: An Anthology of the Best Poems of Countee Cullen*, 104–37. New York: Harper & Row, 1947.

———. "Christ Recrucified." *Kelley's Magazine*, October 1922: 13. Reprinted in Jean Wagner, ed., *Black Poets of the United States: From Paul Laurence Dunbar to Langston Hughes*, 335. Urbana: University of Illinois Press, 1973.

Douglass, Frederick. *Frederick Douglass: Selected Speeches and Writings*. Edited by Philip Foner. Abridged and adapted by Yuval Taylor. The Library of Black America. Chicago: Lawrence Hill Books, 1999.

Du Bois, W. E. B. "The Church and the Negro." *Crisis: A Record of the Darker Races* 6 (October 1913): 291.

———. *The Souls of Black Folk*. 1903. Reprint, New York: Penguin, 1989.

Goatley, David Emmanuel. *Were You There? Godforsakenness in Slave Religion*. The Bishop Henry McNeal Turner/Sojourner Truth Series in Black Religion. Maryknoll, NY: Orbis Books, 1996.

Harper, Frances E. W. *Iola Leroy, or Shadows Uplifted*. 1892. Reprint, College Park, MD: McGrath, 1969.

———. "The Woman's Christian Temperance Union and the Colored Woman." *A. M. E. Church Review* 4 (1888): 313–16.

Hopkins, Dwight N., and George C. L. Cummings, eds. *Cut Loose Your Stammering Tongue: Black Theology in the Slave Narratives*. 2nd ed. Louisville: Westminster John Knox, 2003.

Jacobs, Harriet A. *Incidents in the Life of a Slave Girl, Written by Herself*. Enlarged ed. Edited by Jean Fagan Yellin. Cambridge, MA: Harvard University Press, 2000.

Johnson, James Weldon, and J. Rosamond Johnson. *The Books of American Negro Spirituals*. 1925–26. Reprint, New York: Viking, 1940.

King, Martin Luther, Jr. "Suffering and Faith." *Christian Century* 77 (27 April 1960): 510.

Mathews, Donald G. "Lynching Is Part of the Religion of Our People: Faith in the Christian South." In *Religion in the American South*, edited by Beth Barton Schweiger and Donald G. Mathews, 153–94. Chapel Hill: University of North Carolina Press, 2004.

———. "Lynching Religion: Why the Old Man Shouted 'Glory!'" In *Southern Crossroads: Perspectives on Religion and Culture*, edited by Walter H. Conser Jr. and Rodger M. Payne, 318–53. Religion in the South. Lexington: University Press of Kentucky, 2008.

———. "The Southern Rite of Human Sacrifice." *Journal of Southern Religion* 3 (2000): unpaginated, http://jsr.fsu.edu/mathews.htm.

Parrish, Lydia. *Slave Songs of the Georgia Sea Islands*. New York: Creative Age Press, 1942.

Patterson, Orlando. "Feast of Blood: 'Race,' Religion, and Human Sacrifice in the Postbellum South." Chap. 2 in *Rituals of Blood: Consequences of Slavery in Two American Centuries*. New York: Basic Civitas, 1998.

Pinn, Anthony B. *Why, Lord? Suffering and Evil in Black Theology*. New York: Continuum, 1995. See esp. 21–56.

Raboteau, Albert J. "'The Blood of the Martyrs Is the Seed of Faith': Suffering in the Christianity of American Slaves." In *The Courage to Hope: From Black Suffering to Human Redemption*, edited by Quinton Hosford Dixie and Cornel West, 22–39. Boston: Beacon, 1999. See esp. 37–38.

Religious Folk Songs of the Negro, as Sung on the Plantations, new ed. . . . from the orig. ed. by Thomas P. Fenner. Hampton, VA: Institute Press, 1909.

Smylie, James H. "Countee Cullen's 'The Black Christ.'" *Theology Today* 38 (July 1981): 160–73.

Stowe, Harriet Beecher. *Uncle Tom's Cabin; or, Life among the Lowly*. In *Harriet Beecher Stowe: Three Novels*, 1–519. New York: Library of America, 1982.

———. *A Key to Uncle Tom's Cabin: Presenting the Original Facts and Documents upon Which the Story Is Founded; Together with Corroborative Statements Verifying the Truth of the Work*. Boston: J. P. Jewett, 1853.

Taylor, Yuval, ed. *I was Born a Slave: An Anthology of Classic Slave Narratives*. 2 vols. The Library of Black America. Chicago: Lawrence Hill Books, 1999.

Thurman, Howard. *Deep River and the Negro Spiritual Speaks of Life and Death*. Richmond, IN: Friends United Press, 1975. See esp. 21–23.

―――. *Jesus and the Disinherited*. Nashville: Abingdon, 1949.

―――. "Suffering." In *Disciplines of the Spirit*, 64–85. Richmond, IN: Friends United Press, 1963. Reprinted in Anthony B. Pinn, ed. *Moral Evil and Redemptive Suffering: A History of Theodicy in African-American Thought*, 227–45. Gainesville: University Press of Florida, 2002.

Truth, Sojourner. *Narrative of Sojourner Truth*. Introduction and notes by Imani Perry. New York: Barnes & Noble Classics, 2005.

Turner, Henry McNeal. "God Is a Negro." In *Respect Black: The Writings and Speeches of Henry McNeal Turner*, 176–77. The American Negro: His History and Literature. New York: Arno Press / *The New York Times*, 1971.

Unwritten History of Slavery: Autobiographical Account of Negro Ex-Slaves. Social Science Source Documents. Nashville: Social Science Institute, Fisk University, 1945.

Wellford, E. T. *The Lynching of Jesus: A Review of the Legal Aspects of the Trial of Christ*. Newport News, VA: Franklin Printing, 1905.

Yetman, Norman R. *Life Under the "Peculiar Institution": Selections from the Slave Narrative Collection*. Huntington, NY: Robert E. Krieger, 1976.

Index